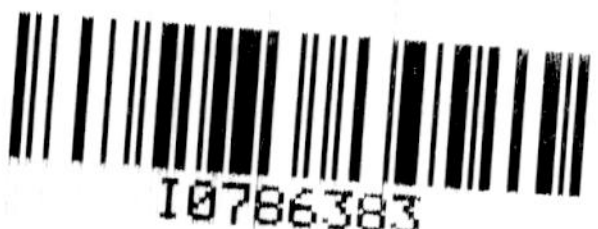

Sacred
Mandala

Copyright: Published in the United States by Peter Raymond
Published August 2018
ISBN-13: 978-1724790712
ISBN-10: 1724790714

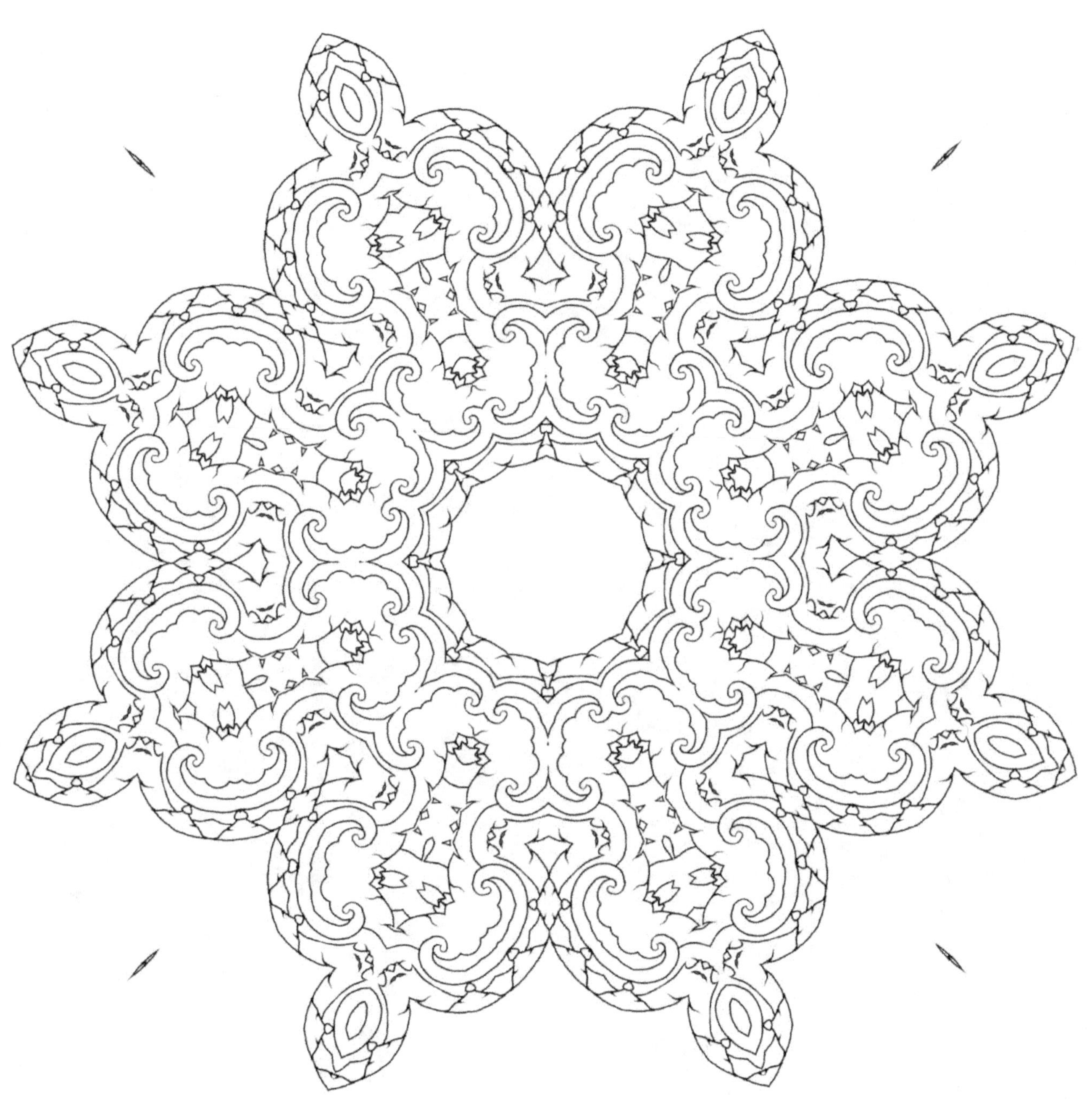

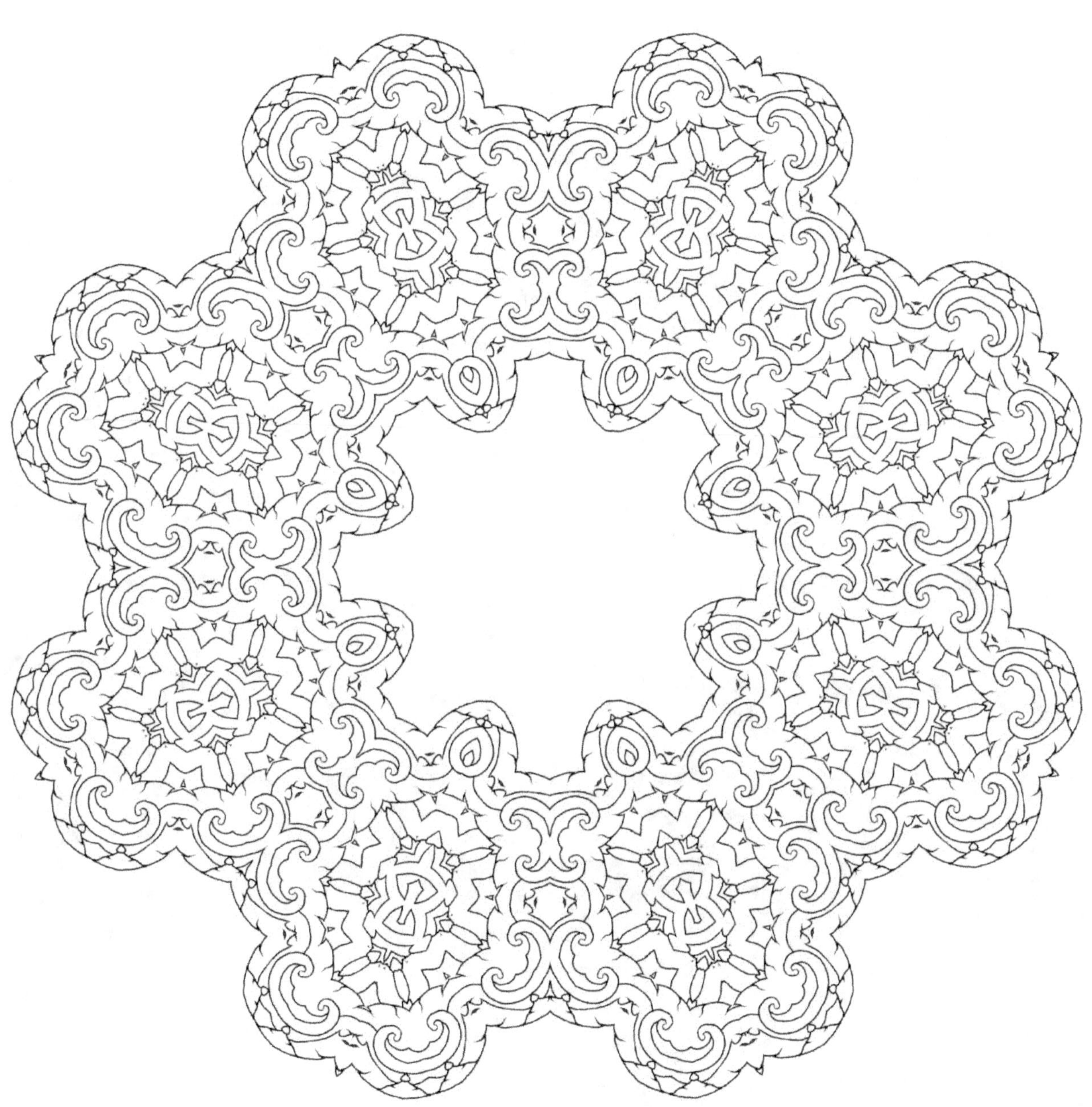

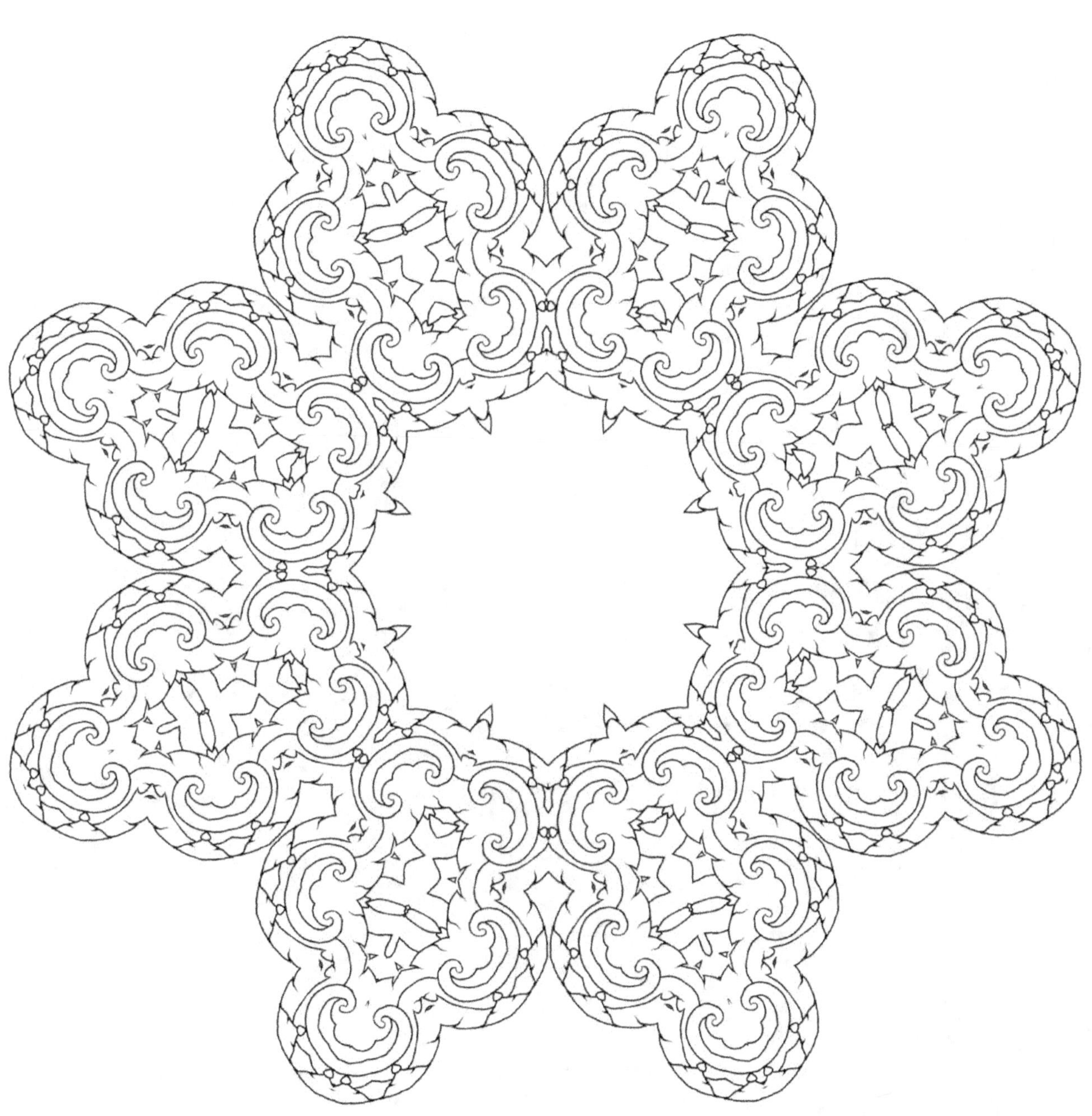

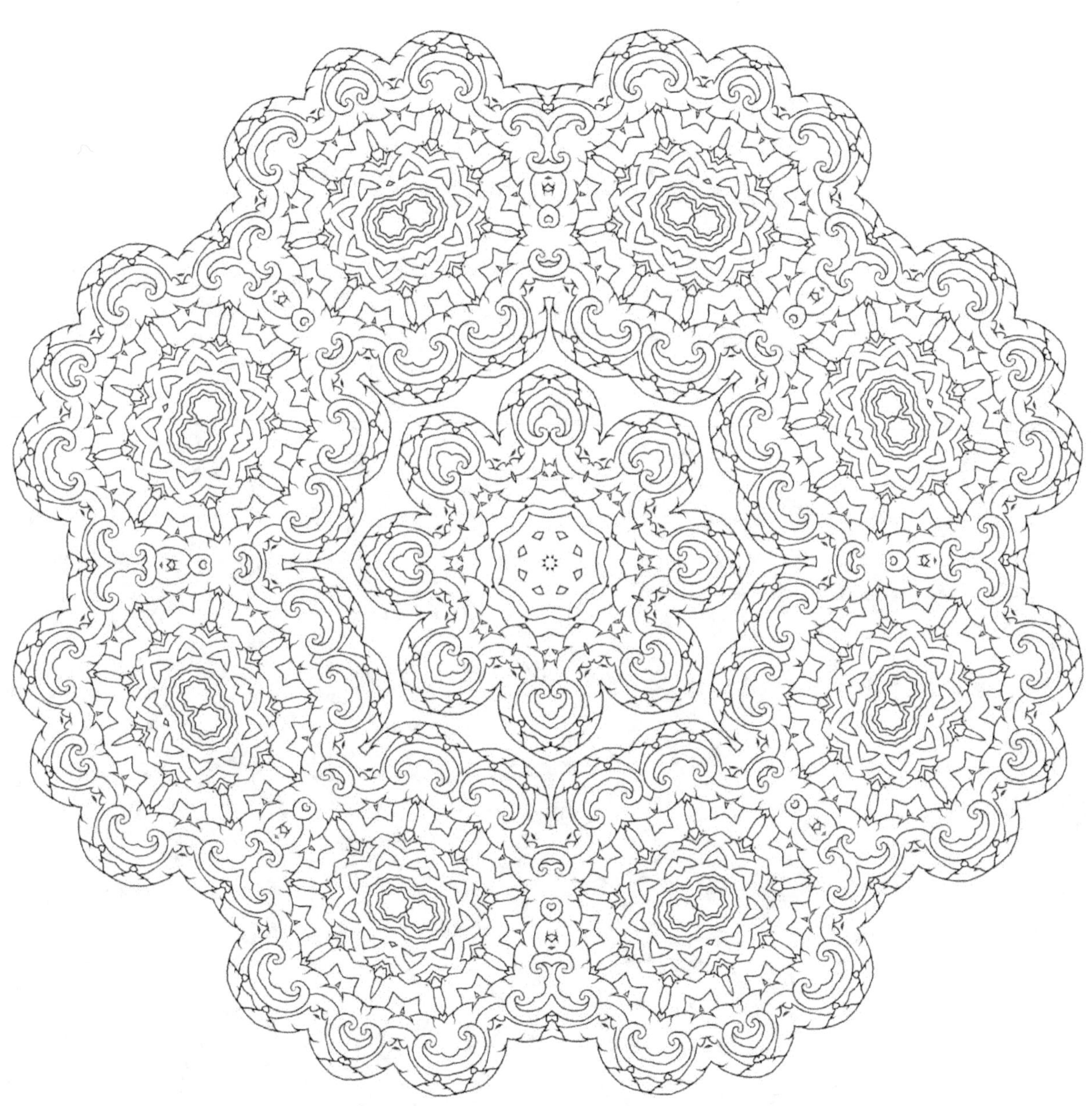

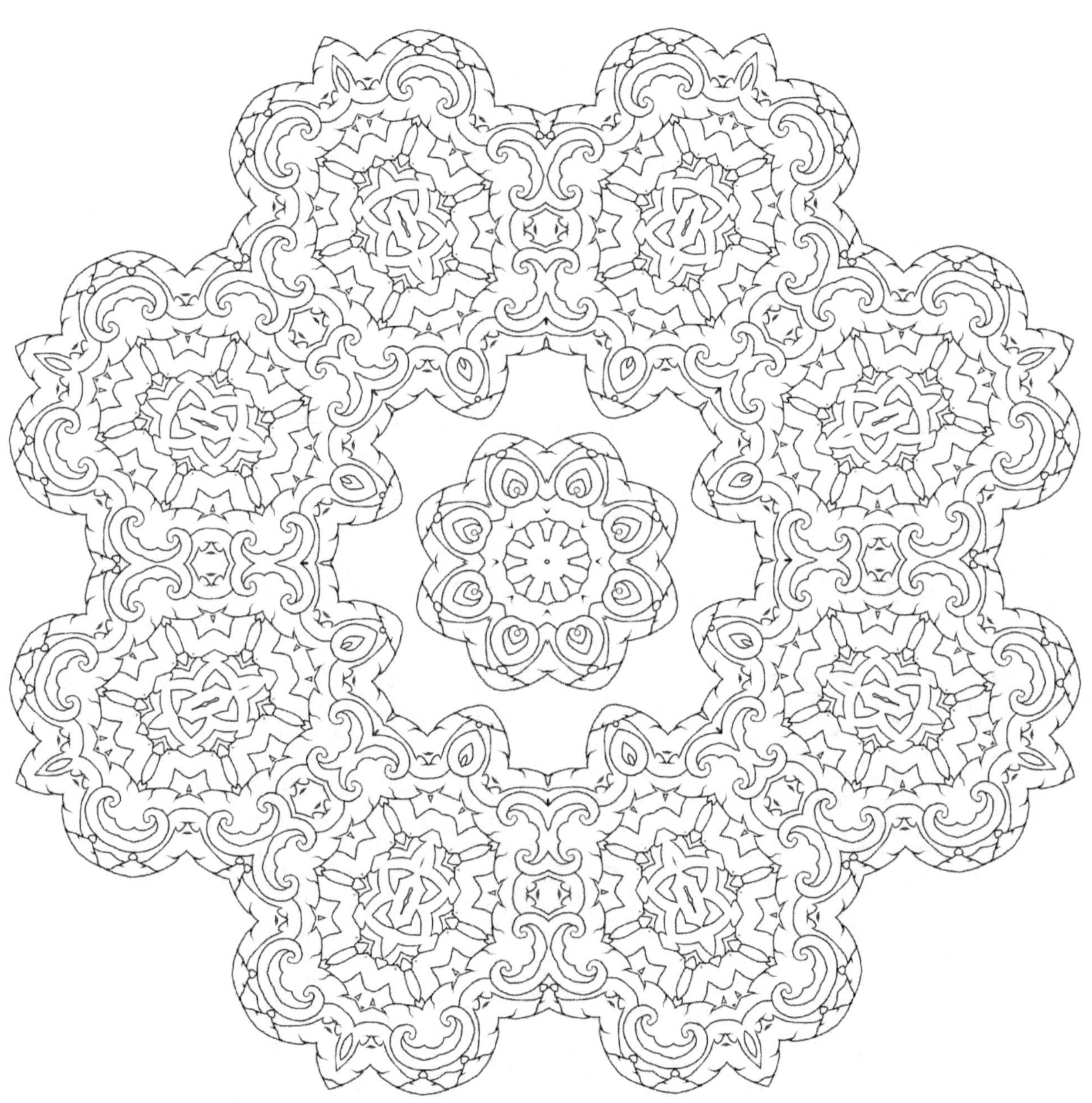

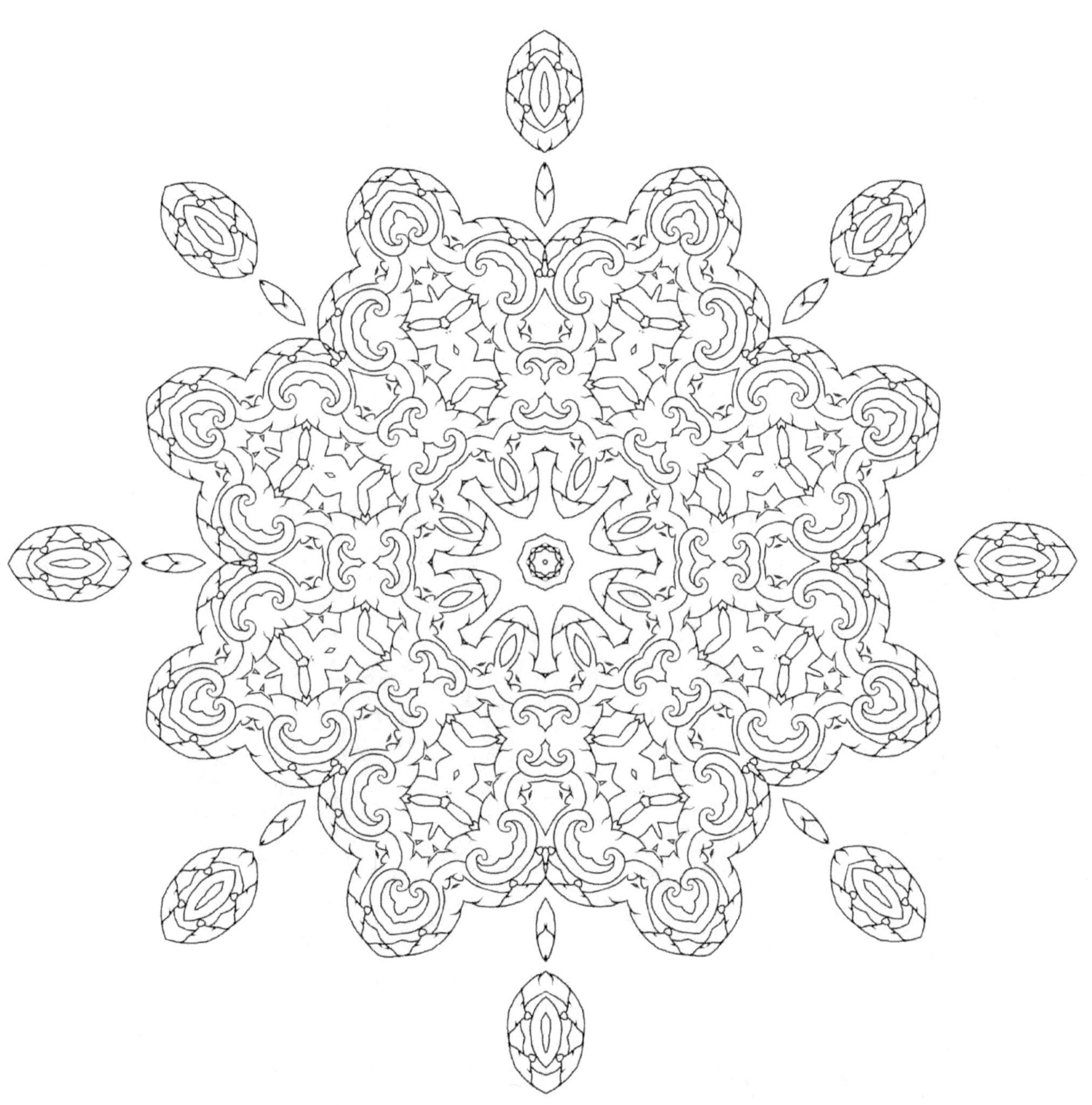

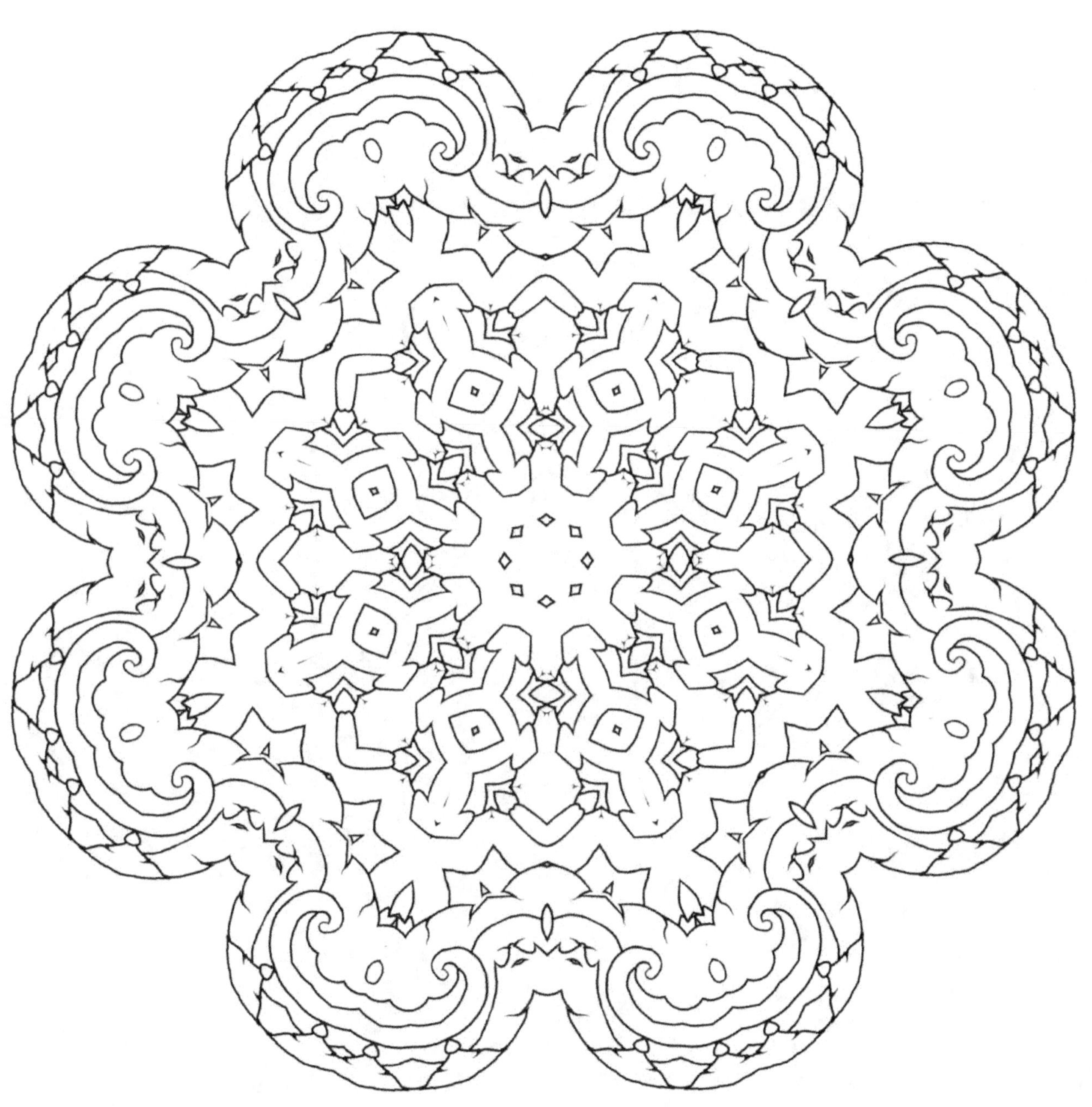

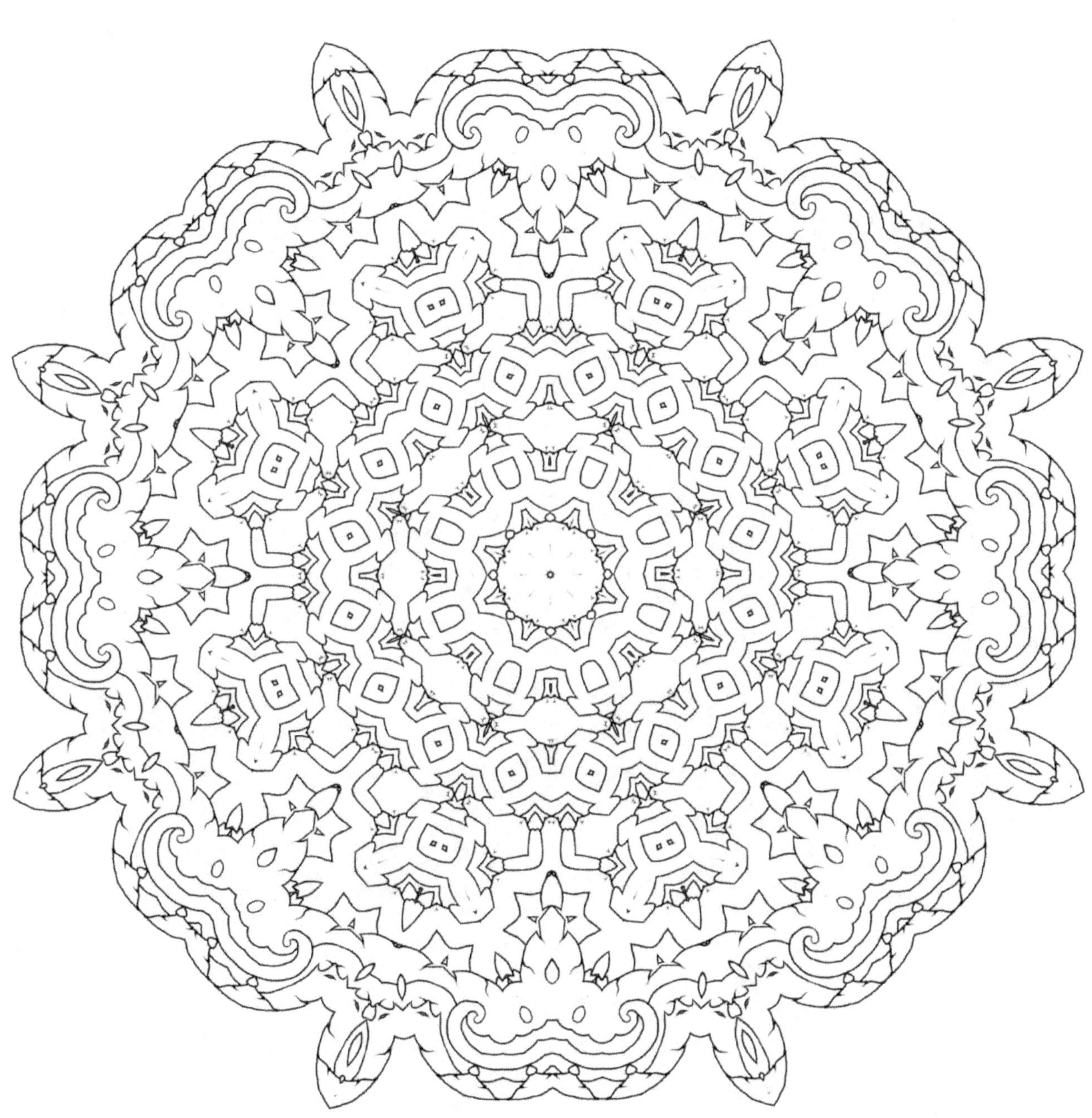

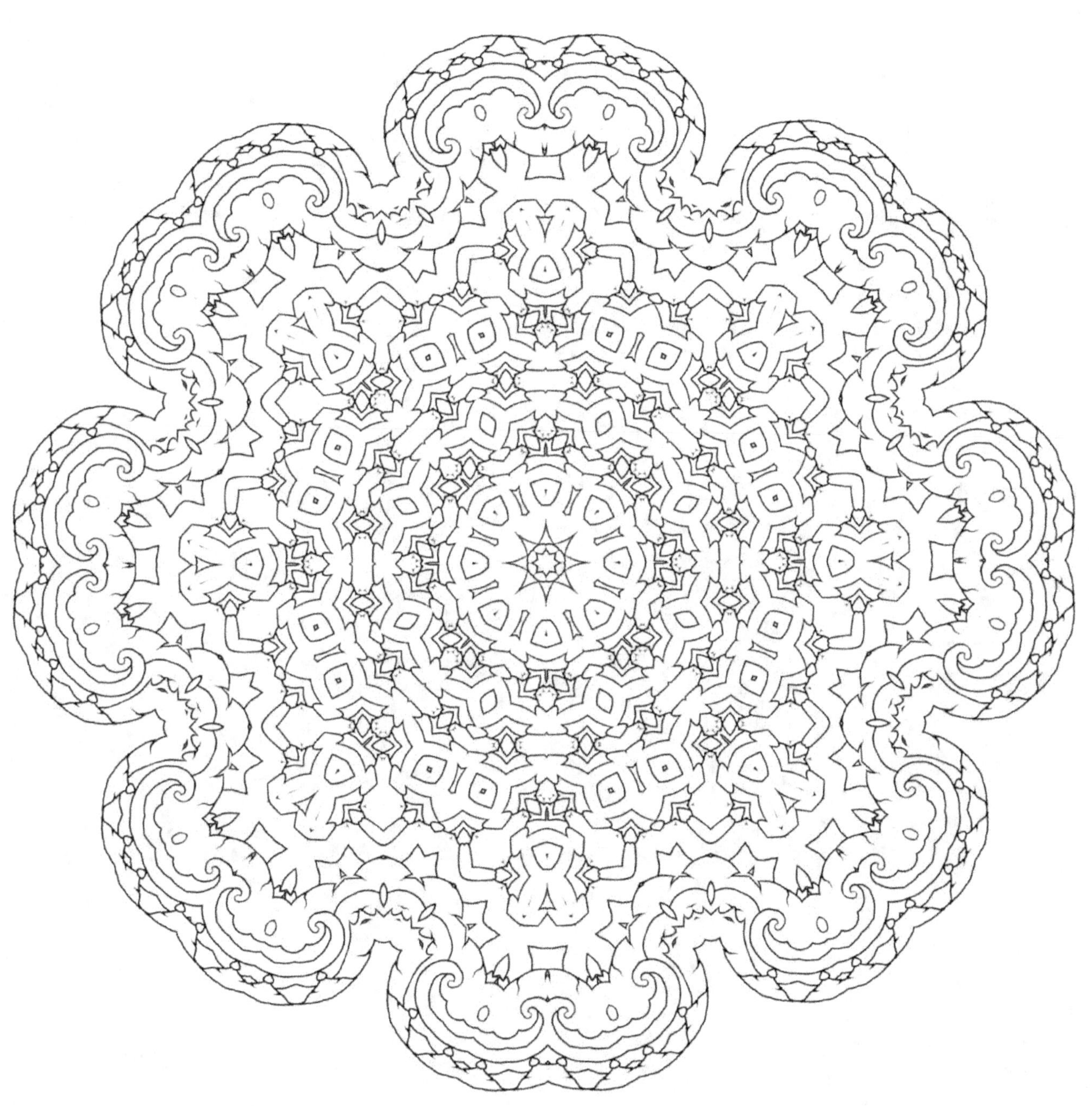

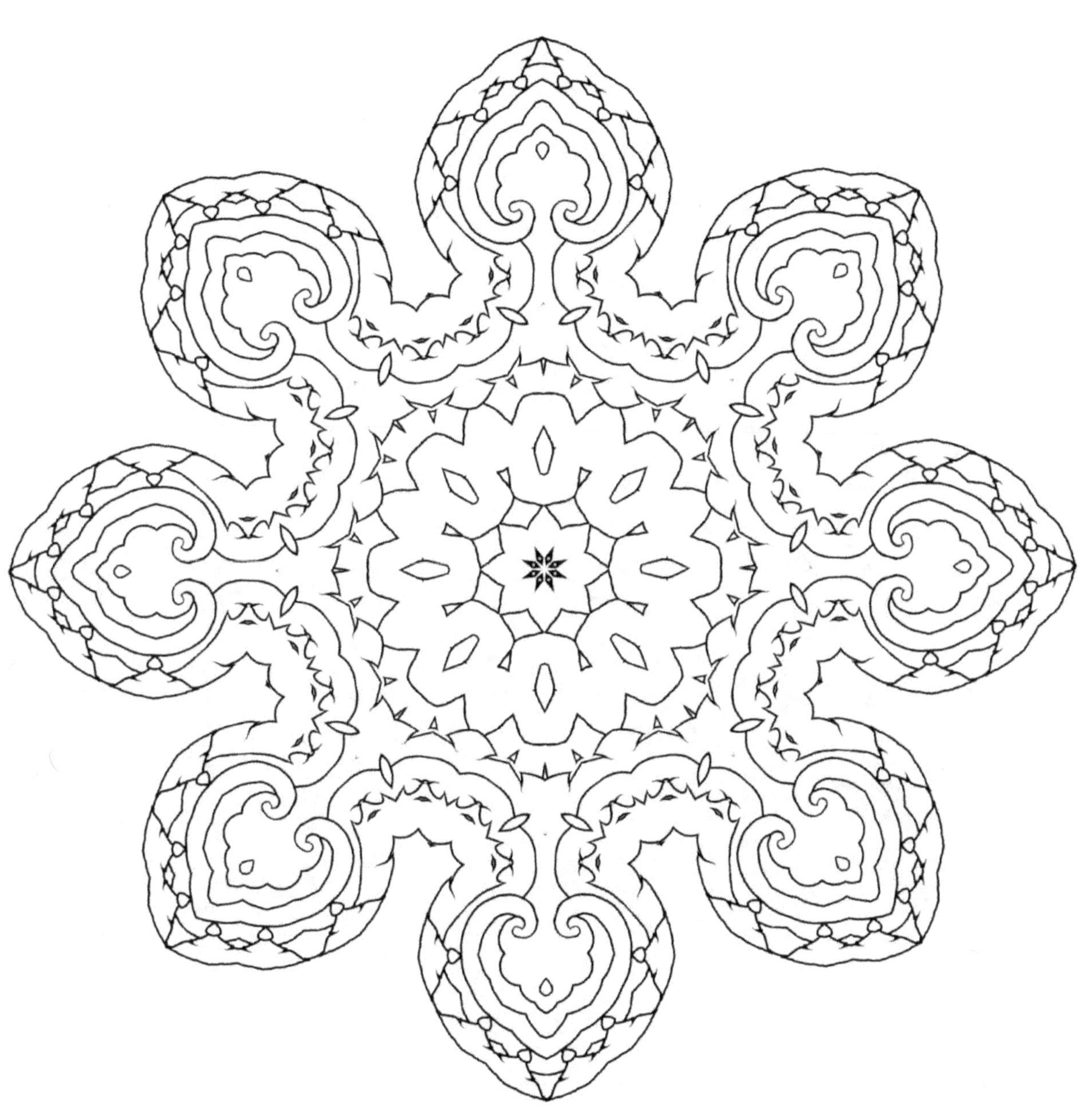

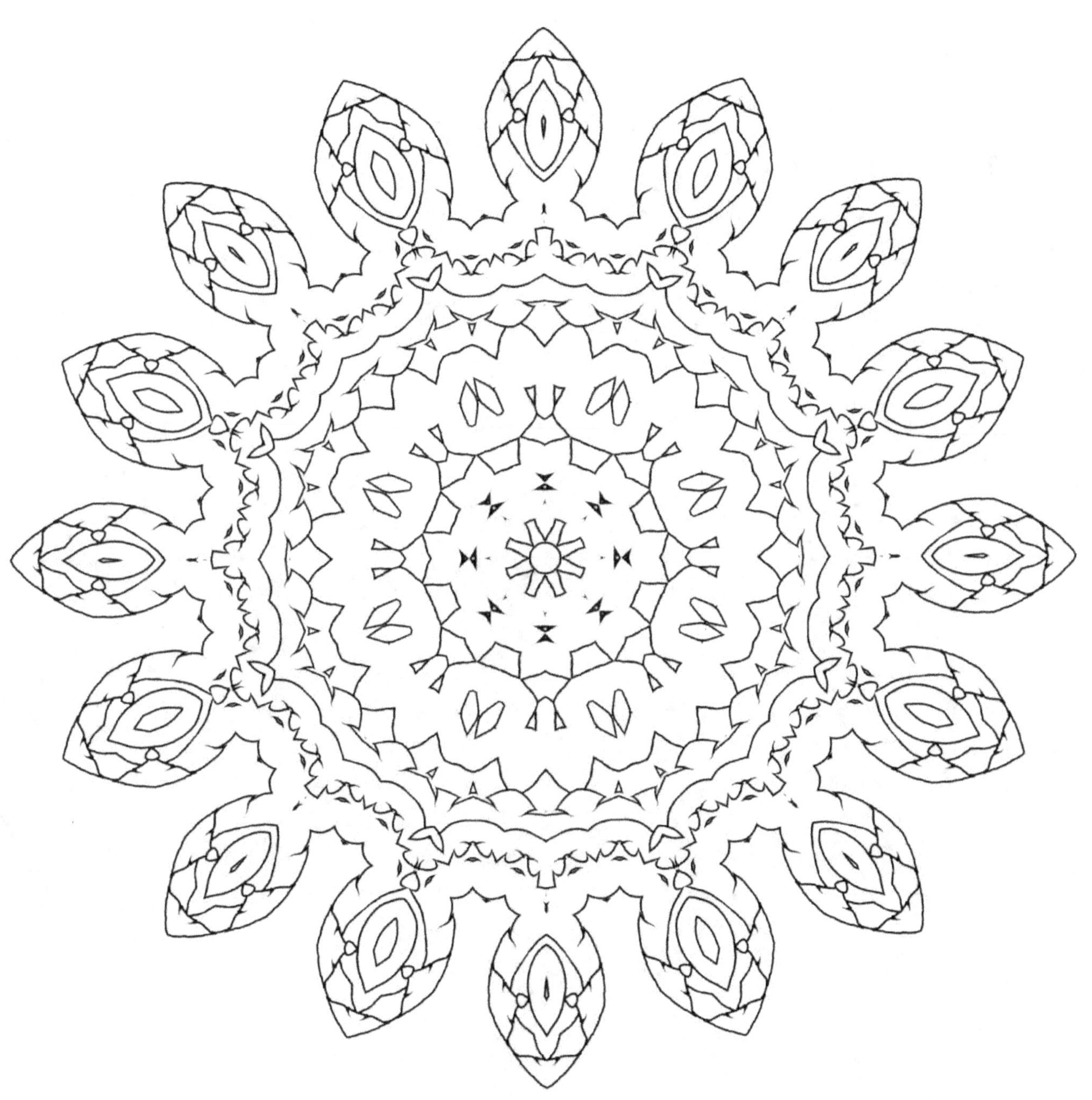

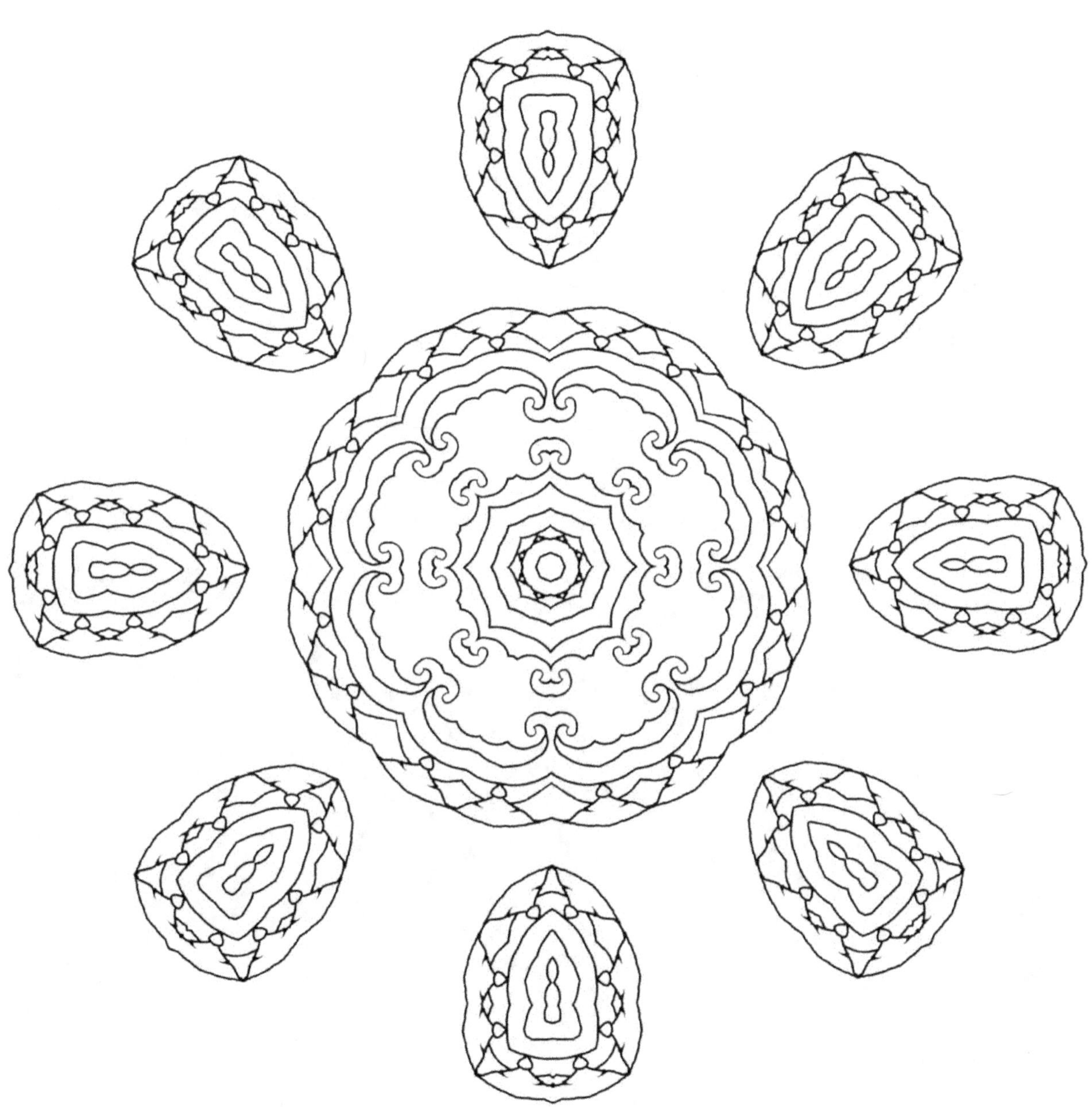

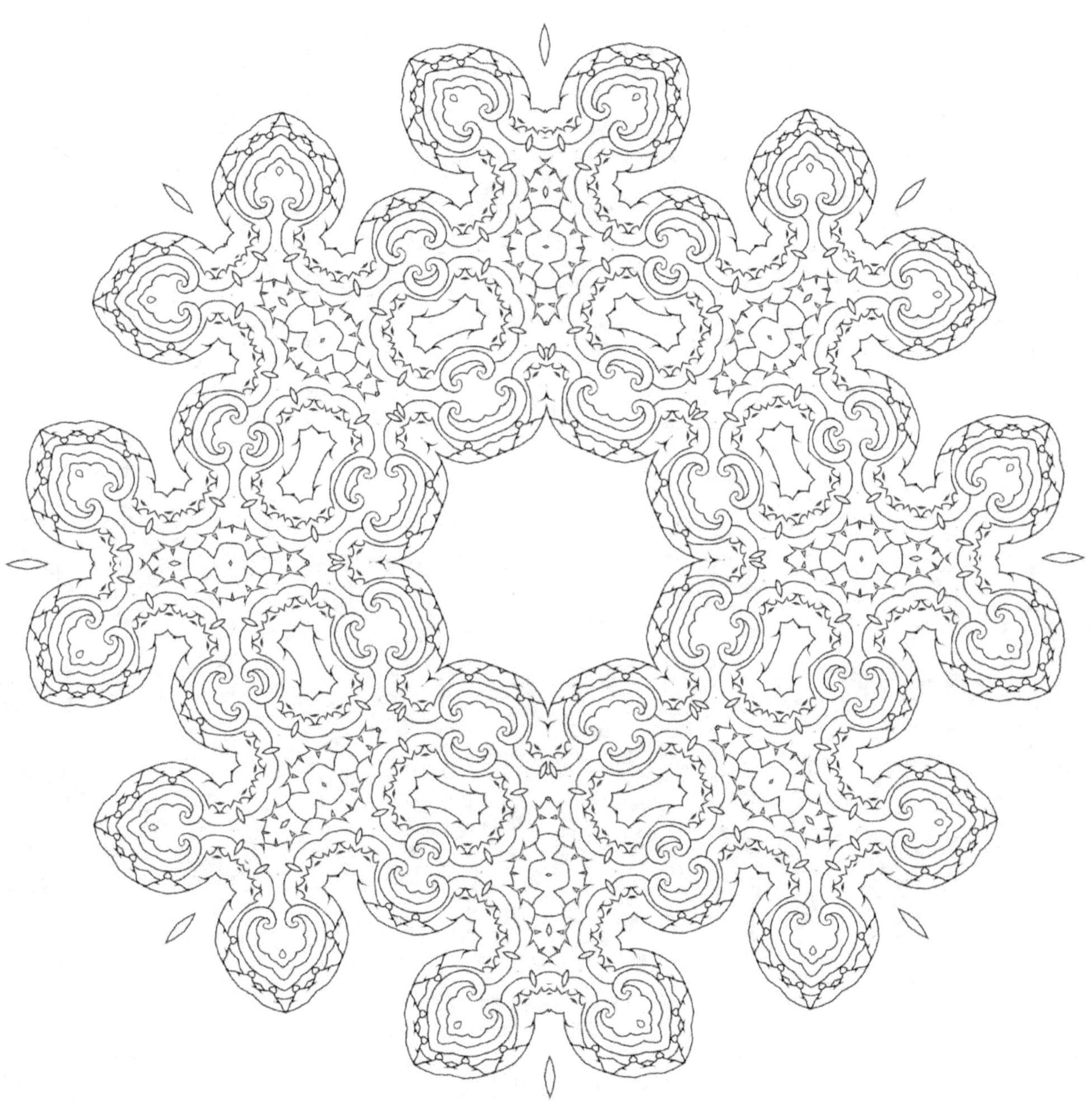

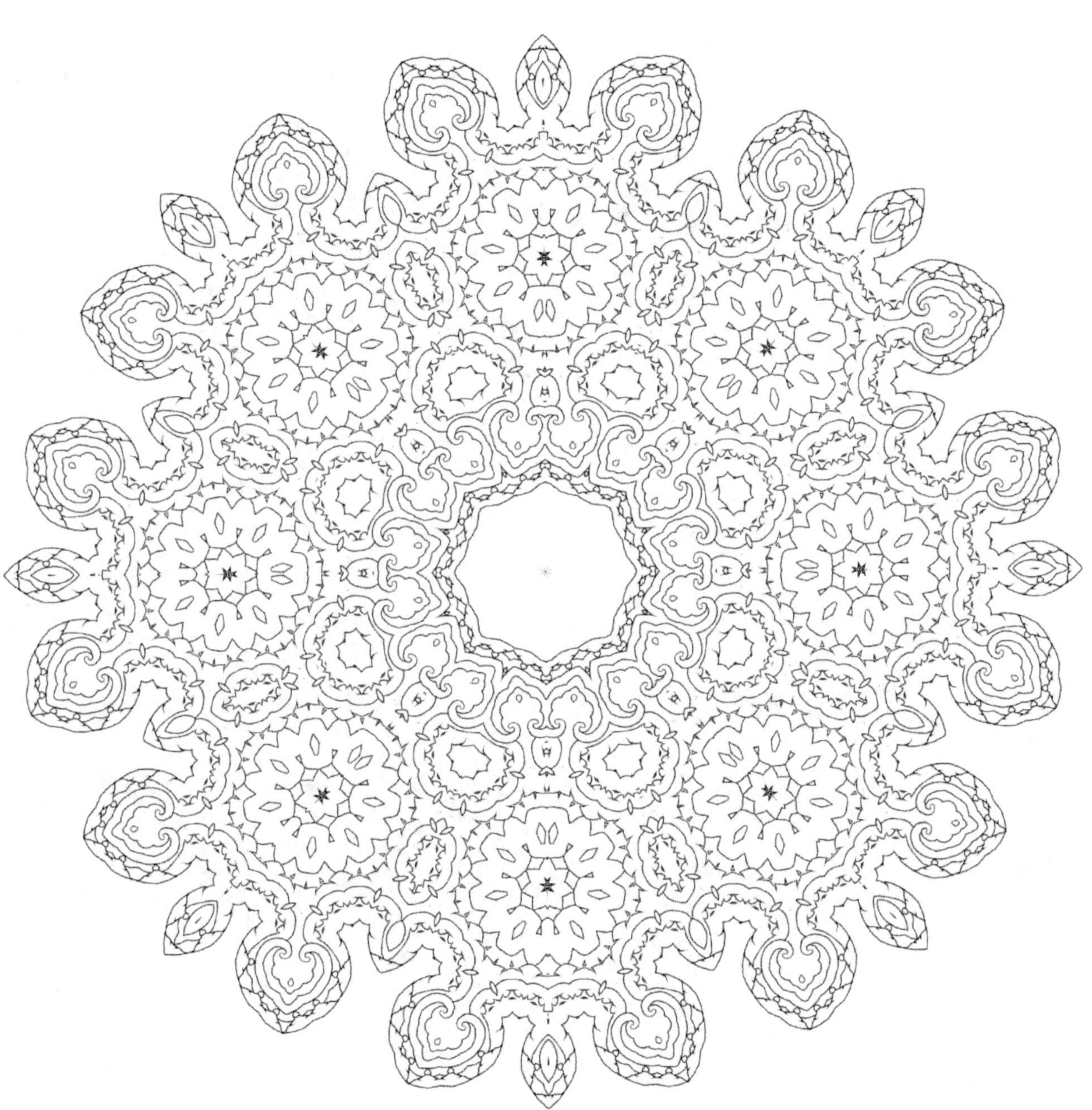

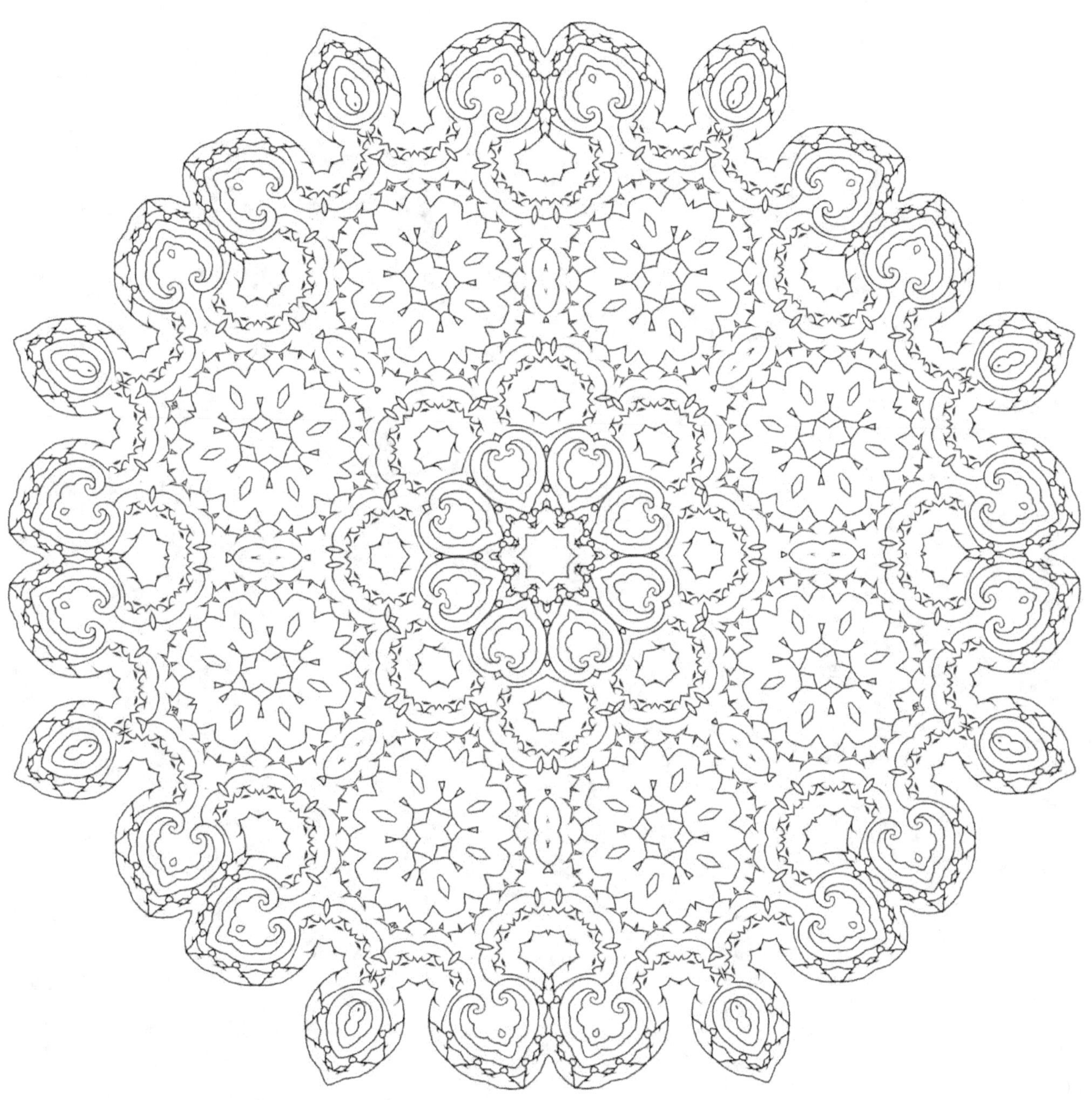

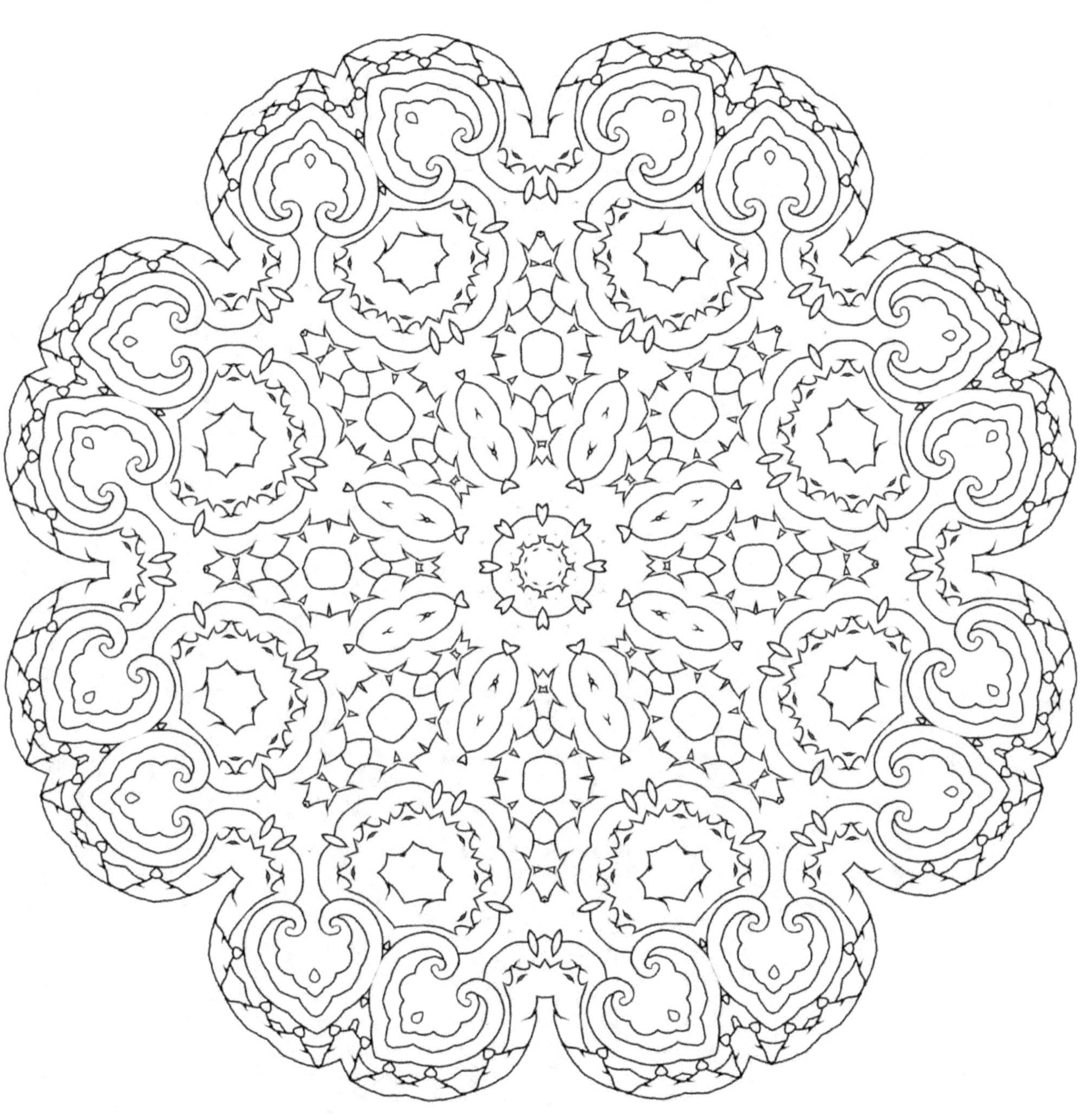

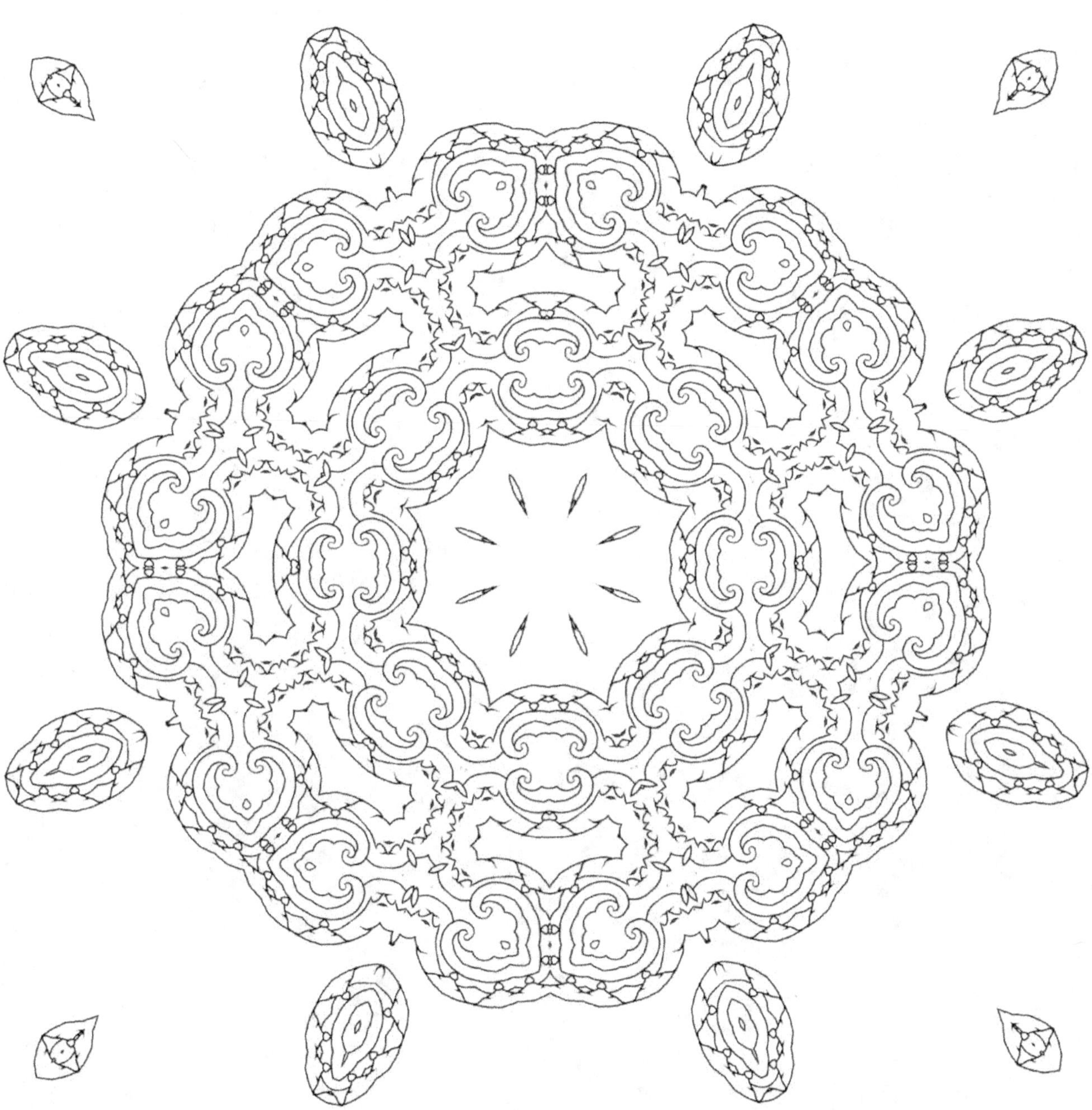

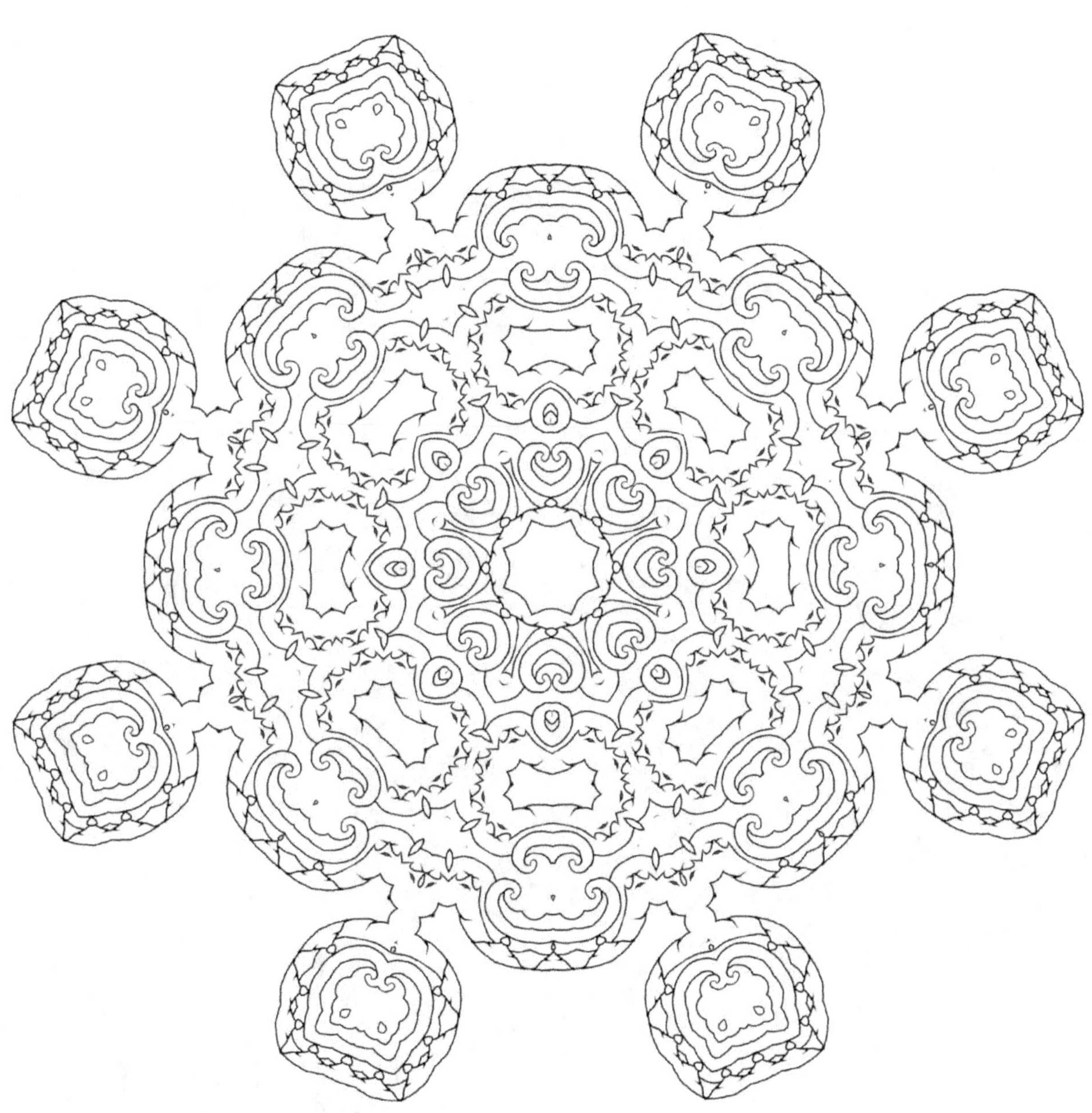

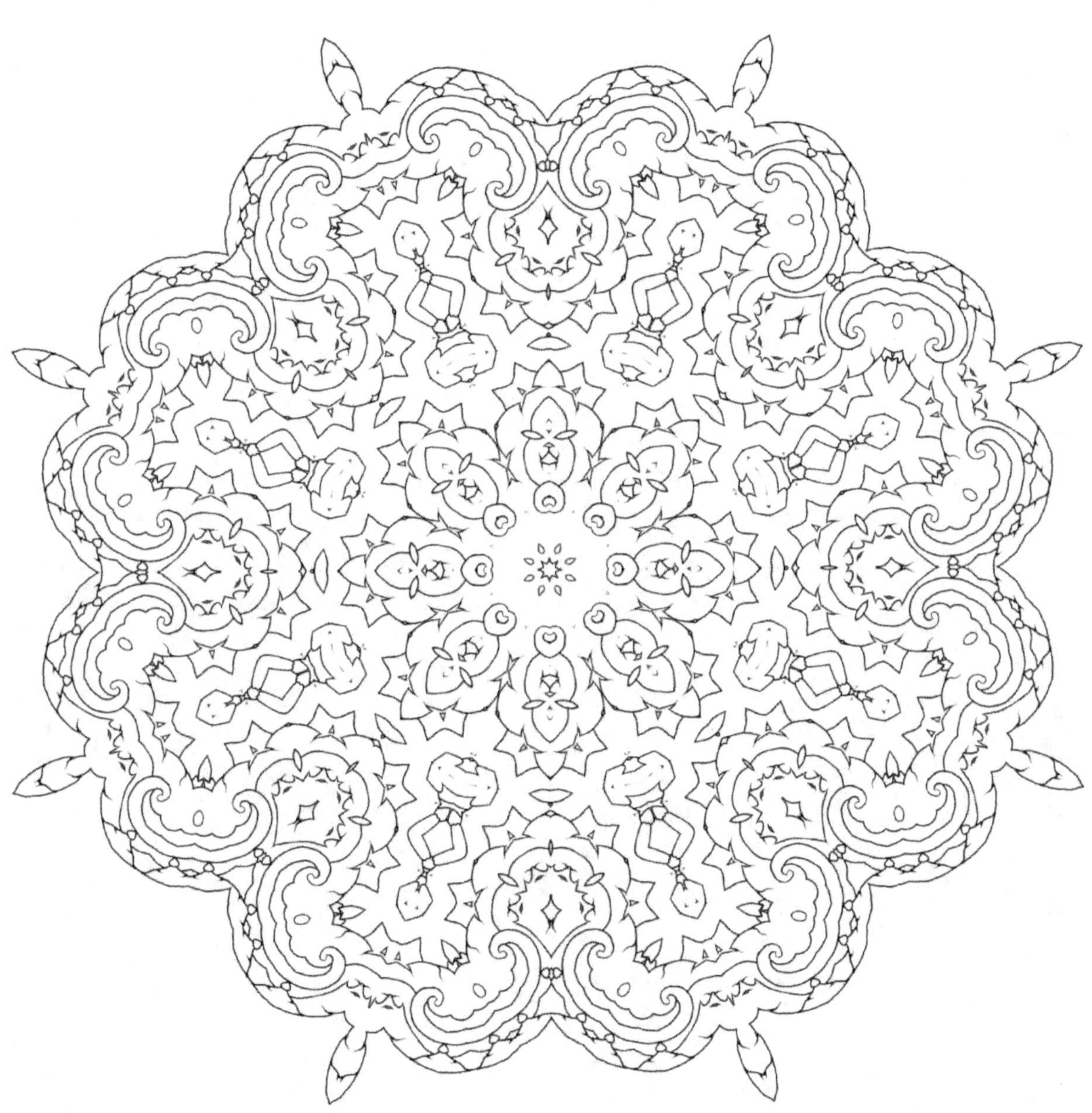

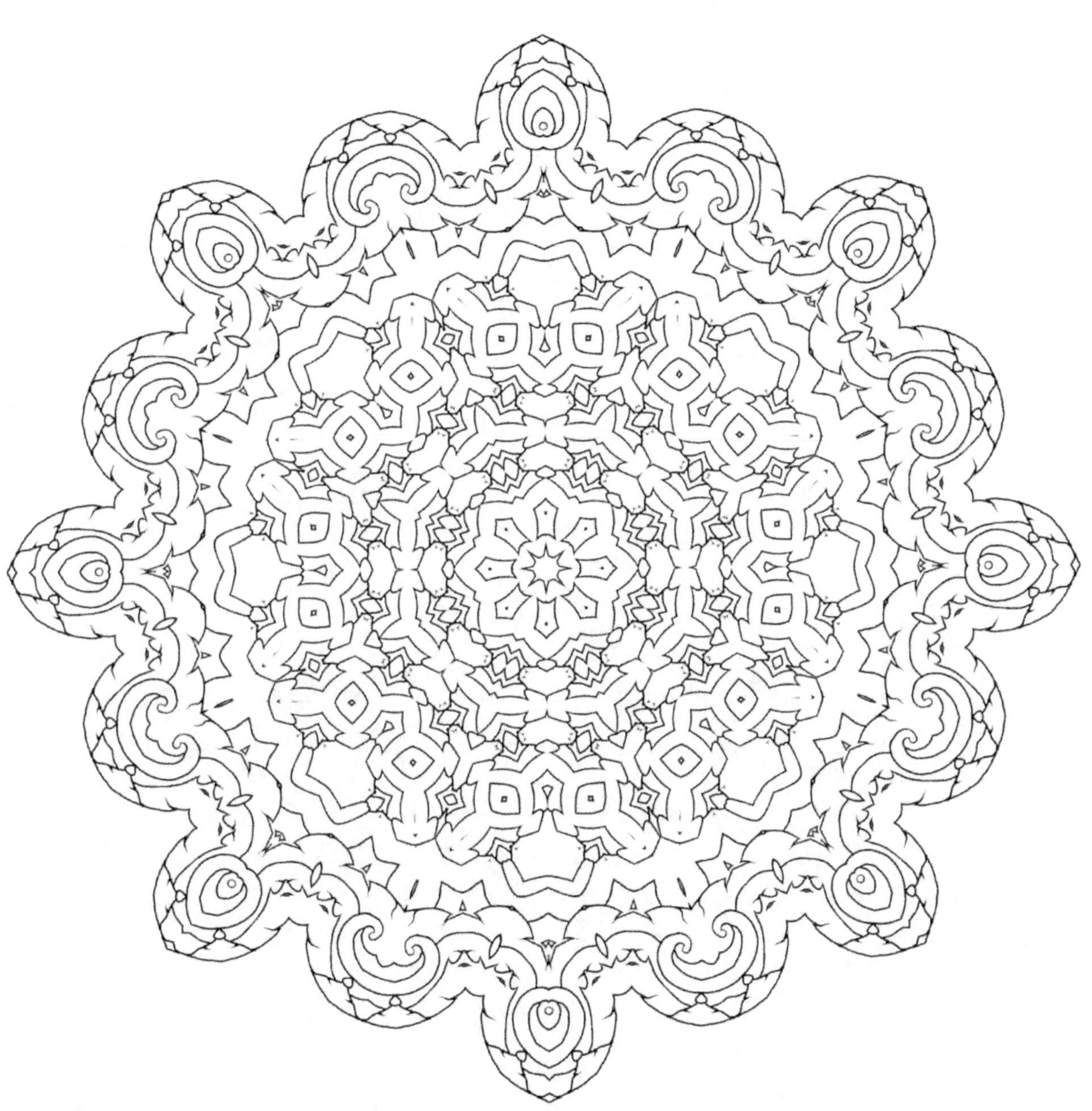

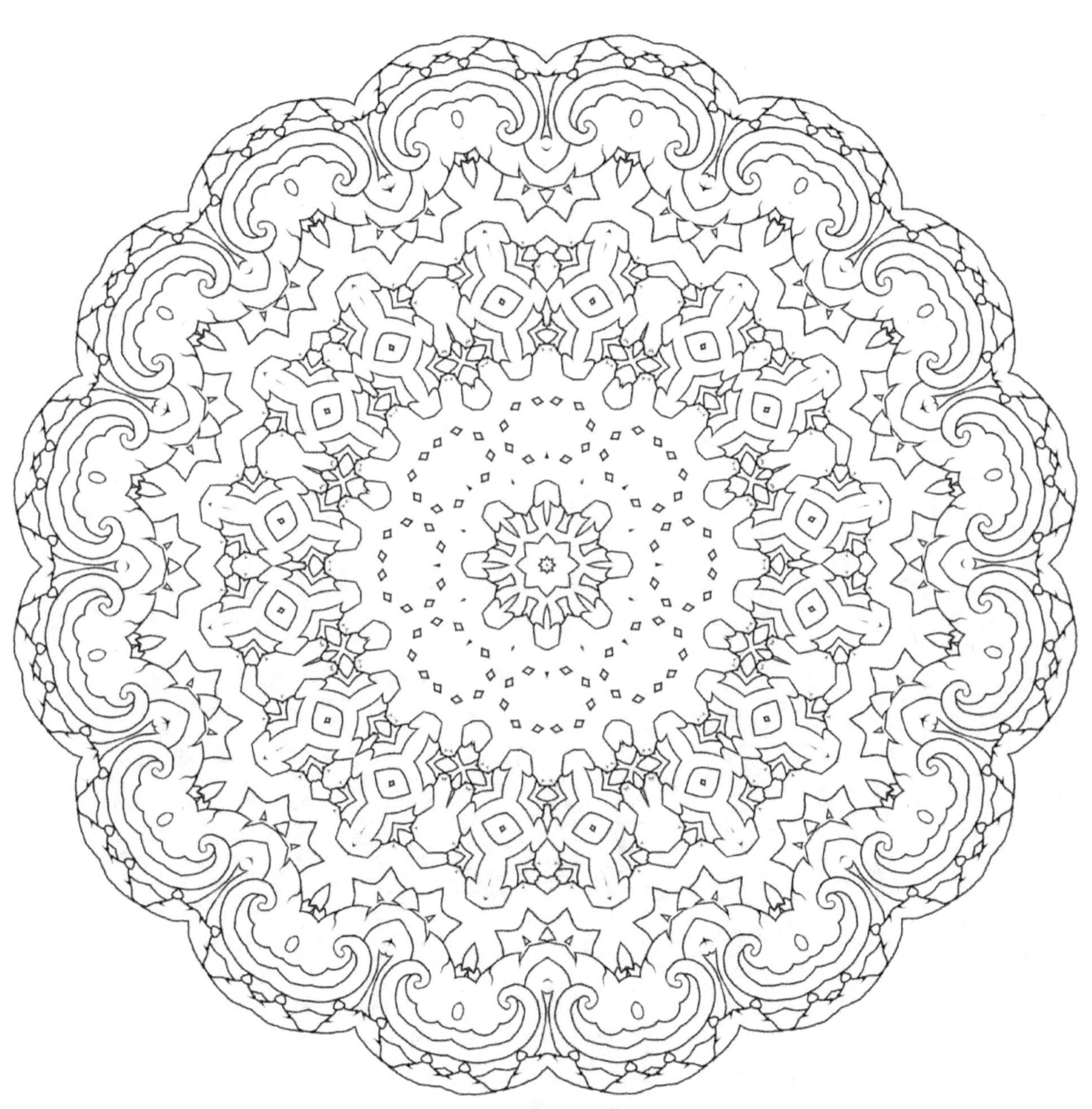

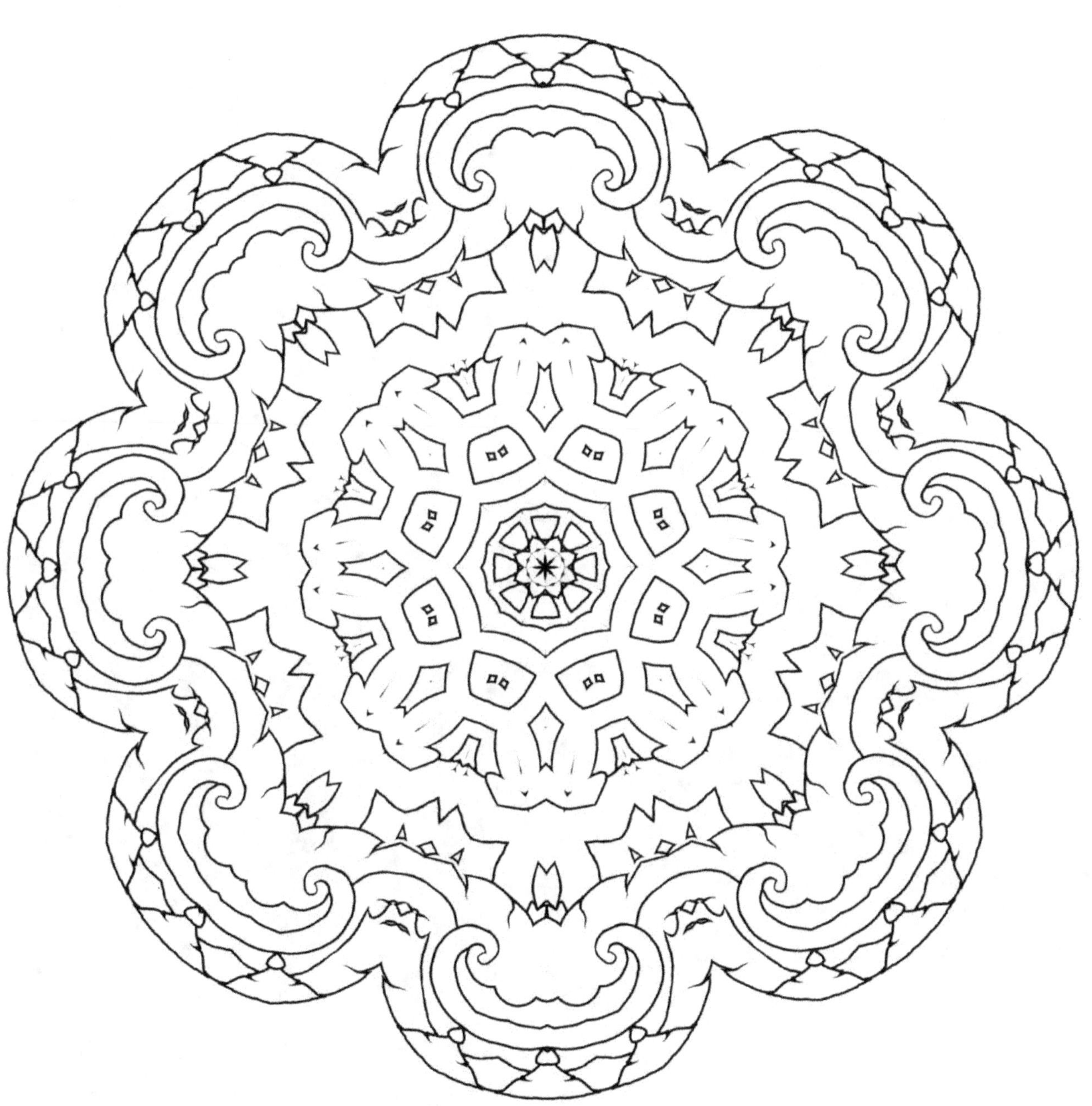

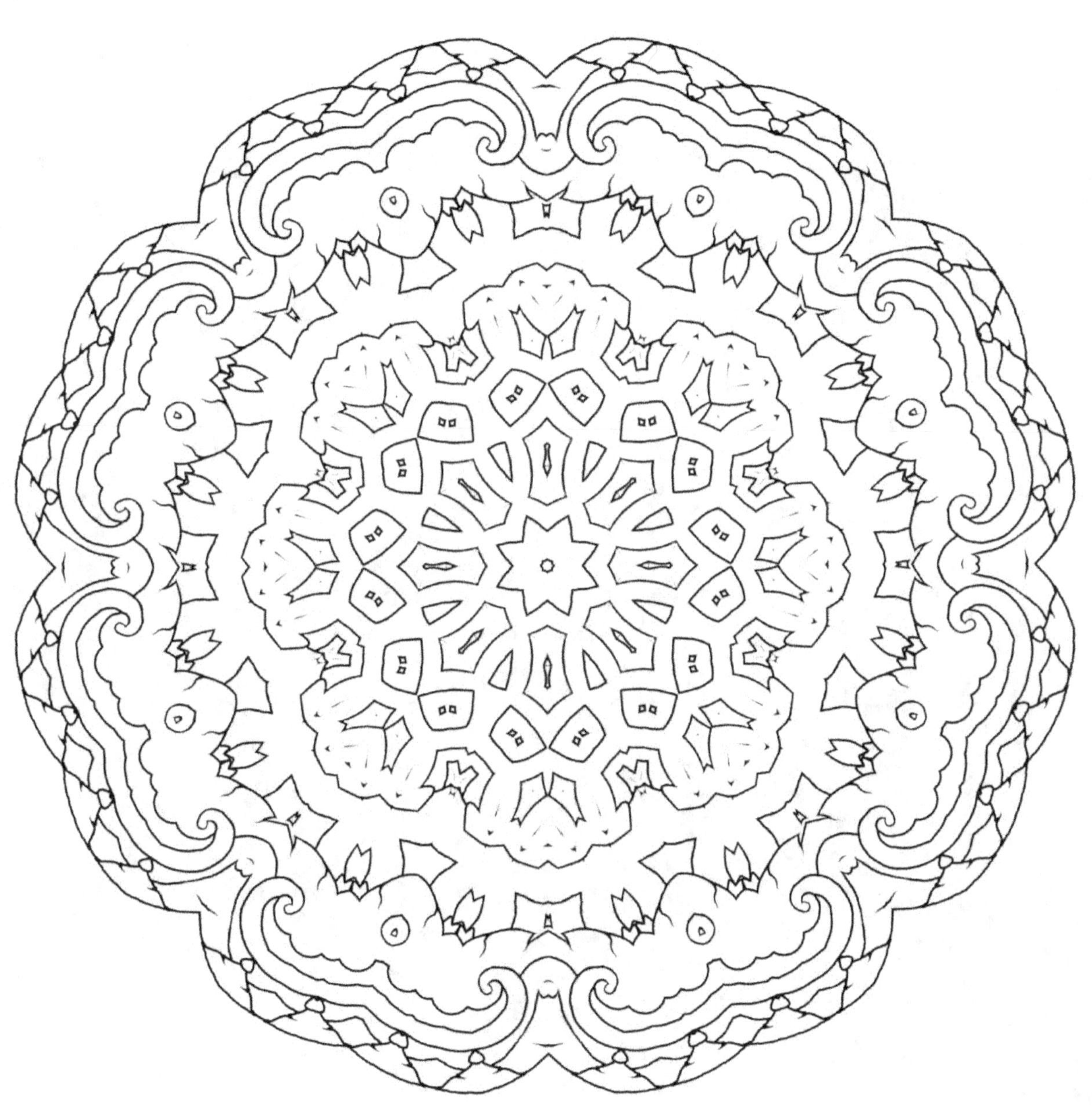

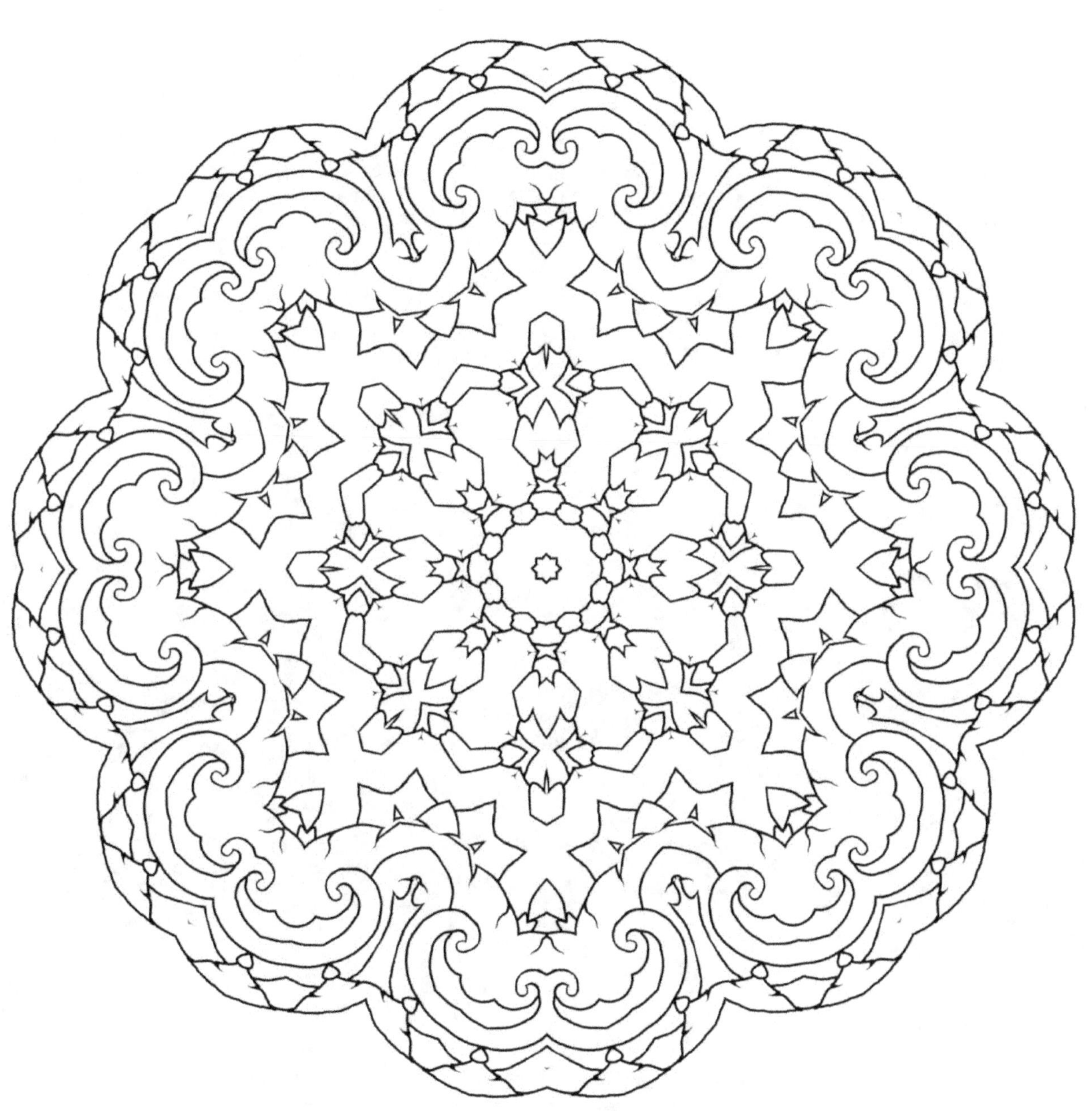

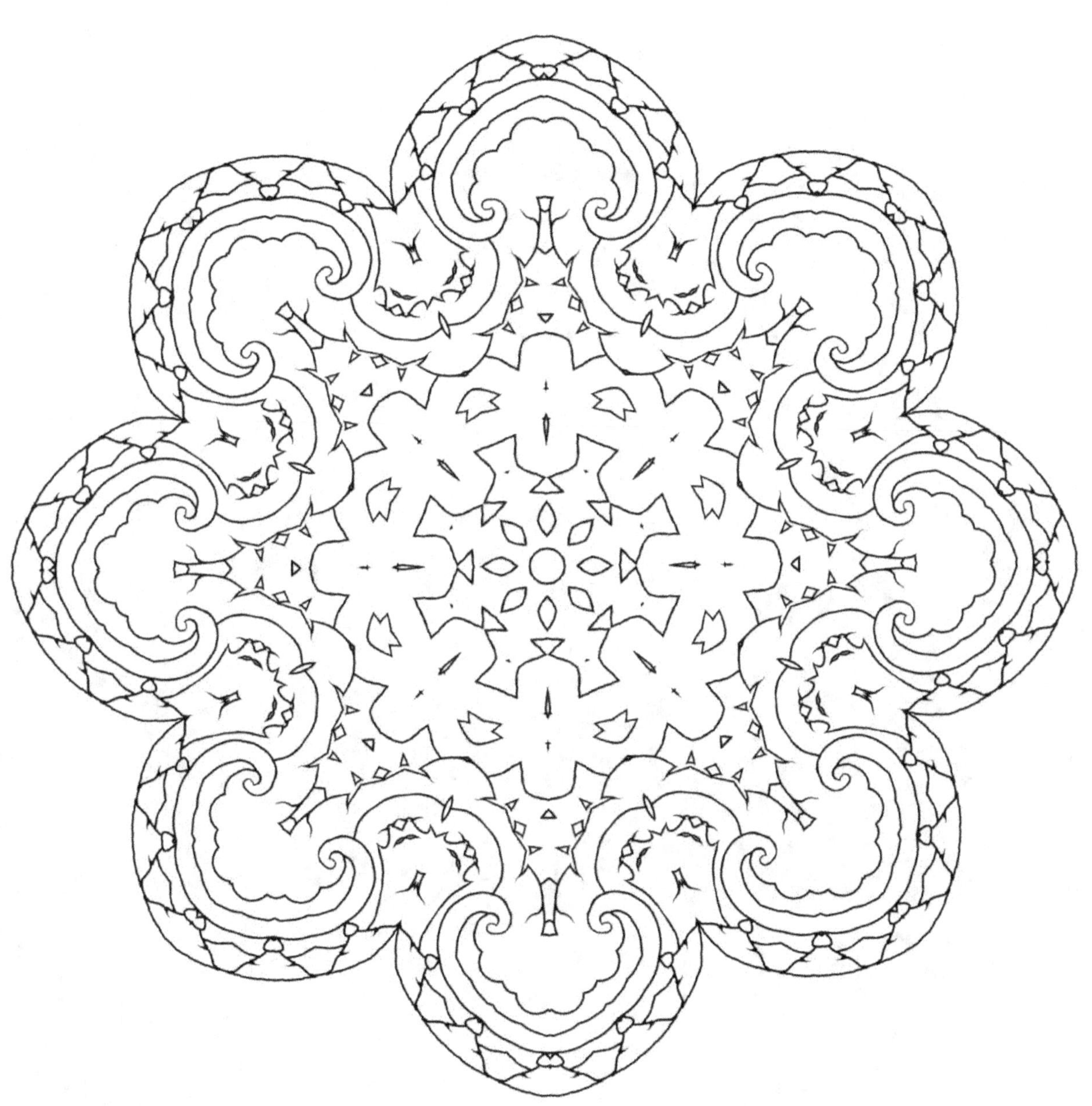

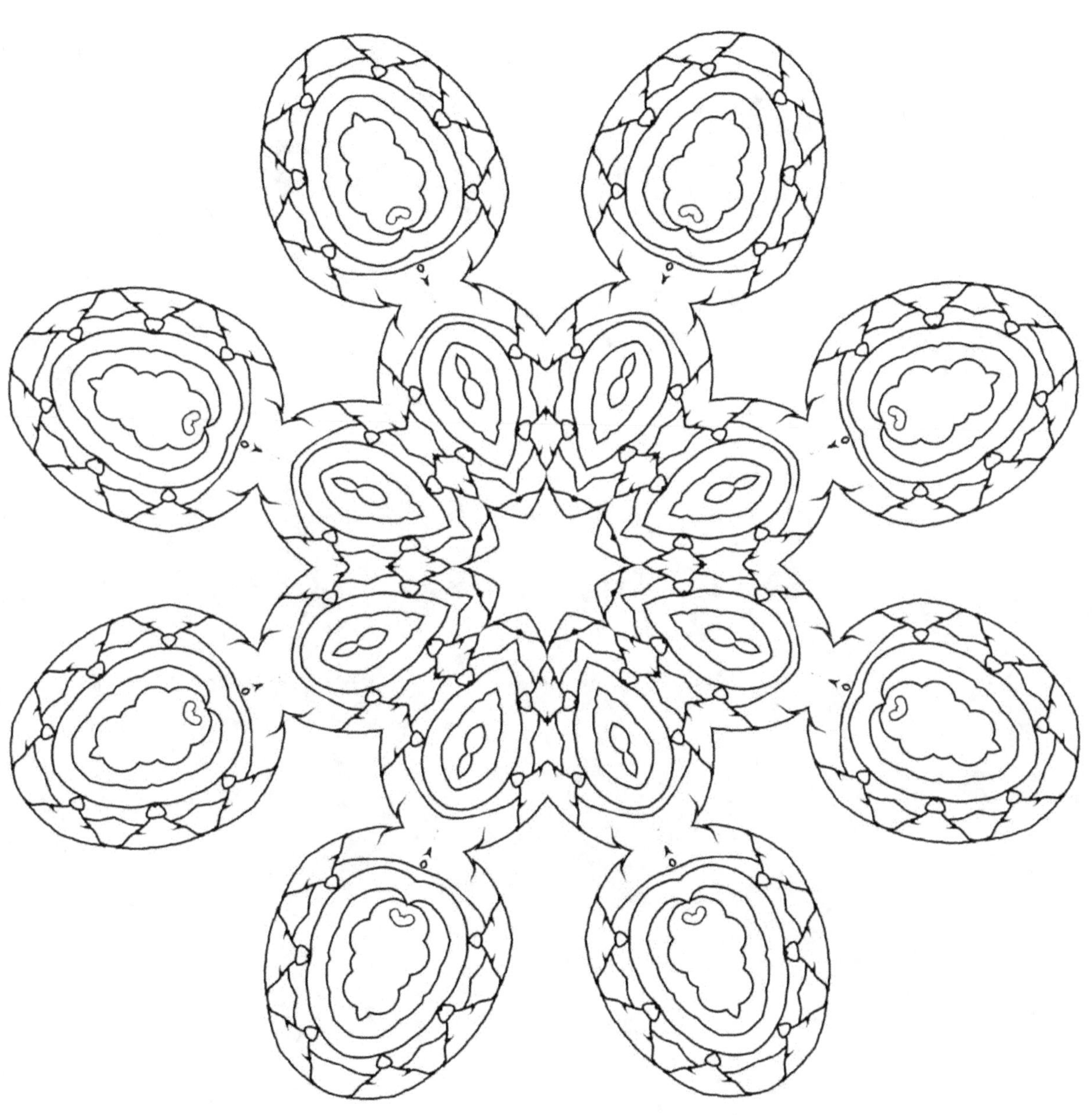

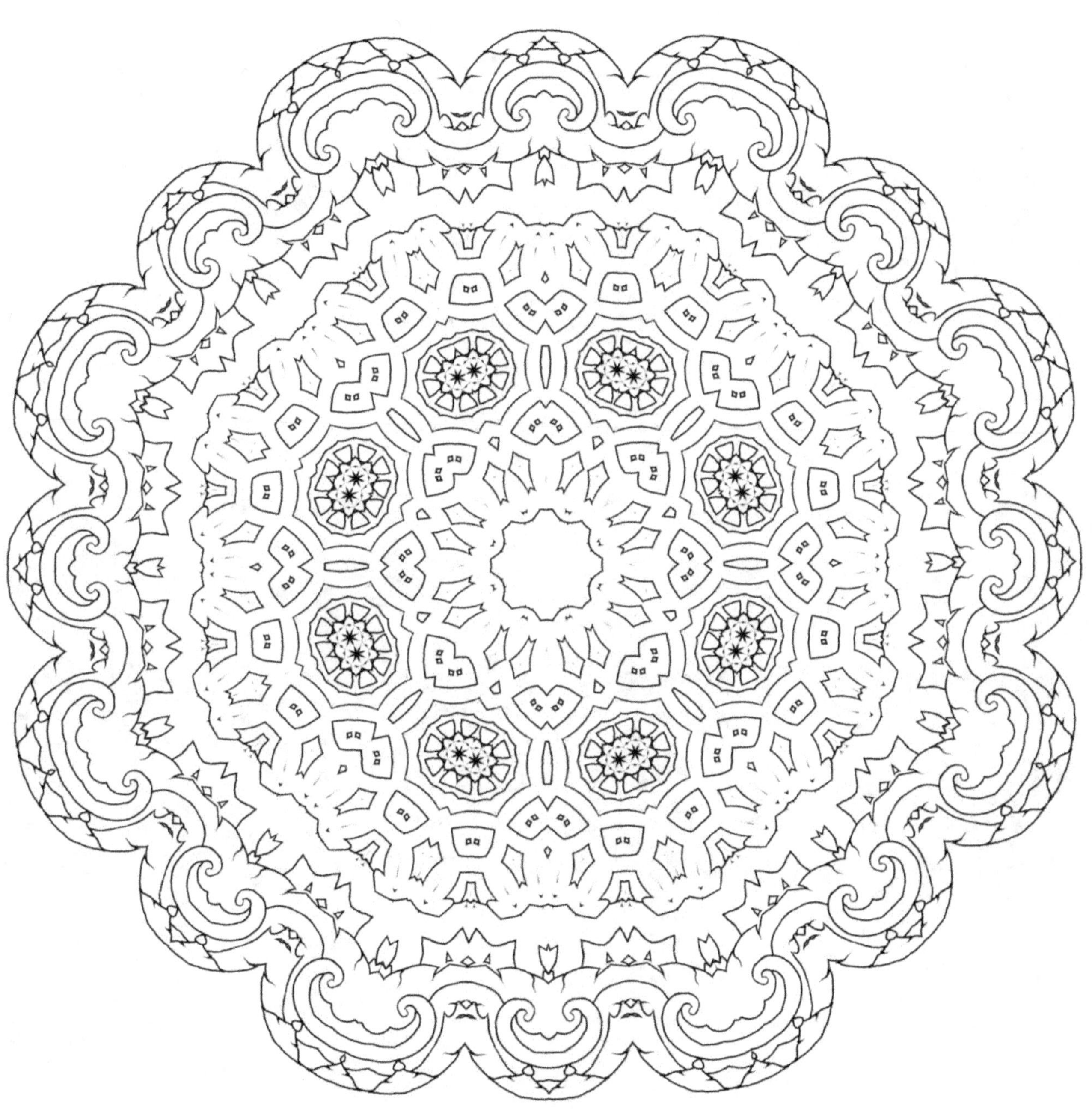

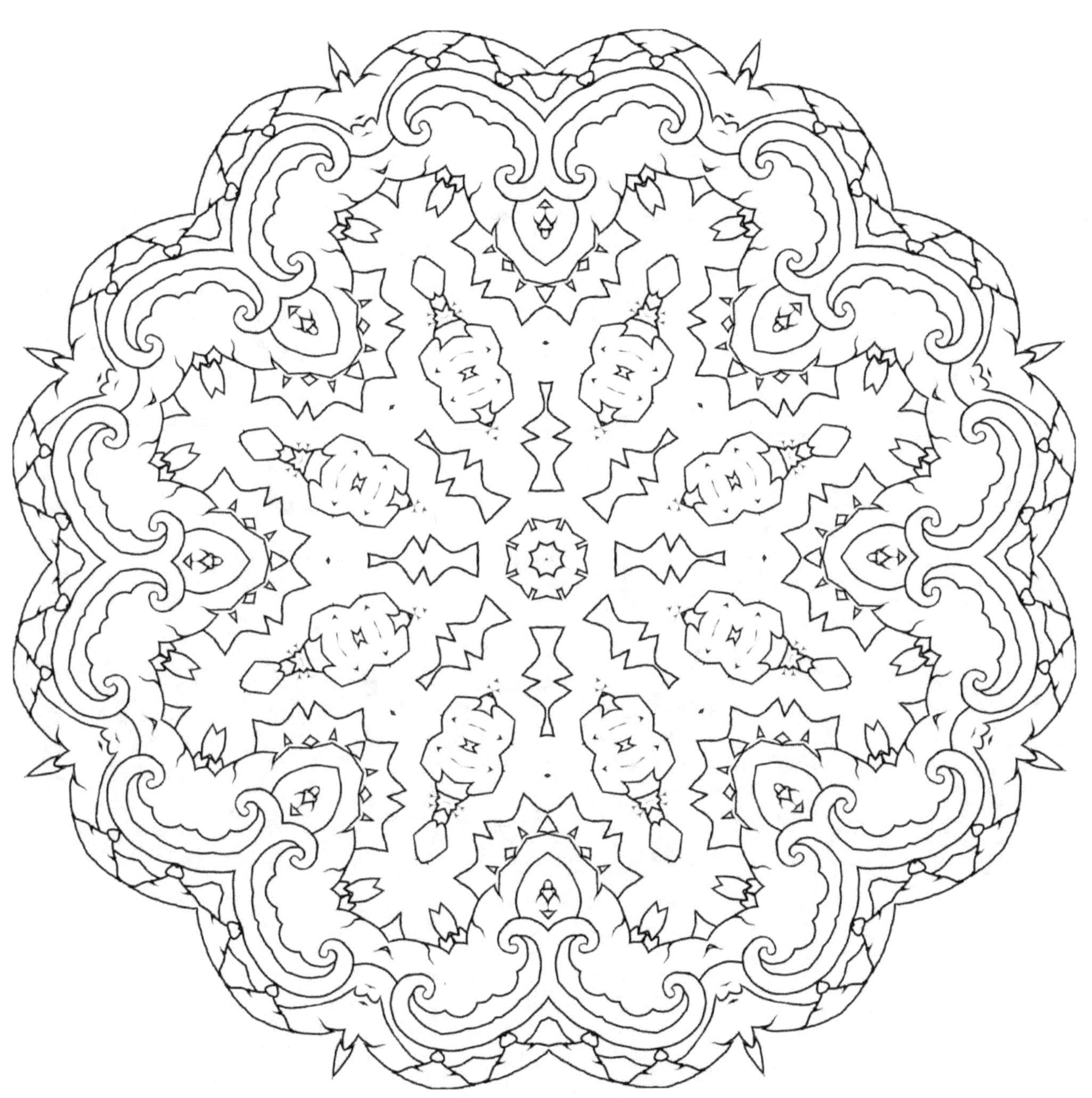

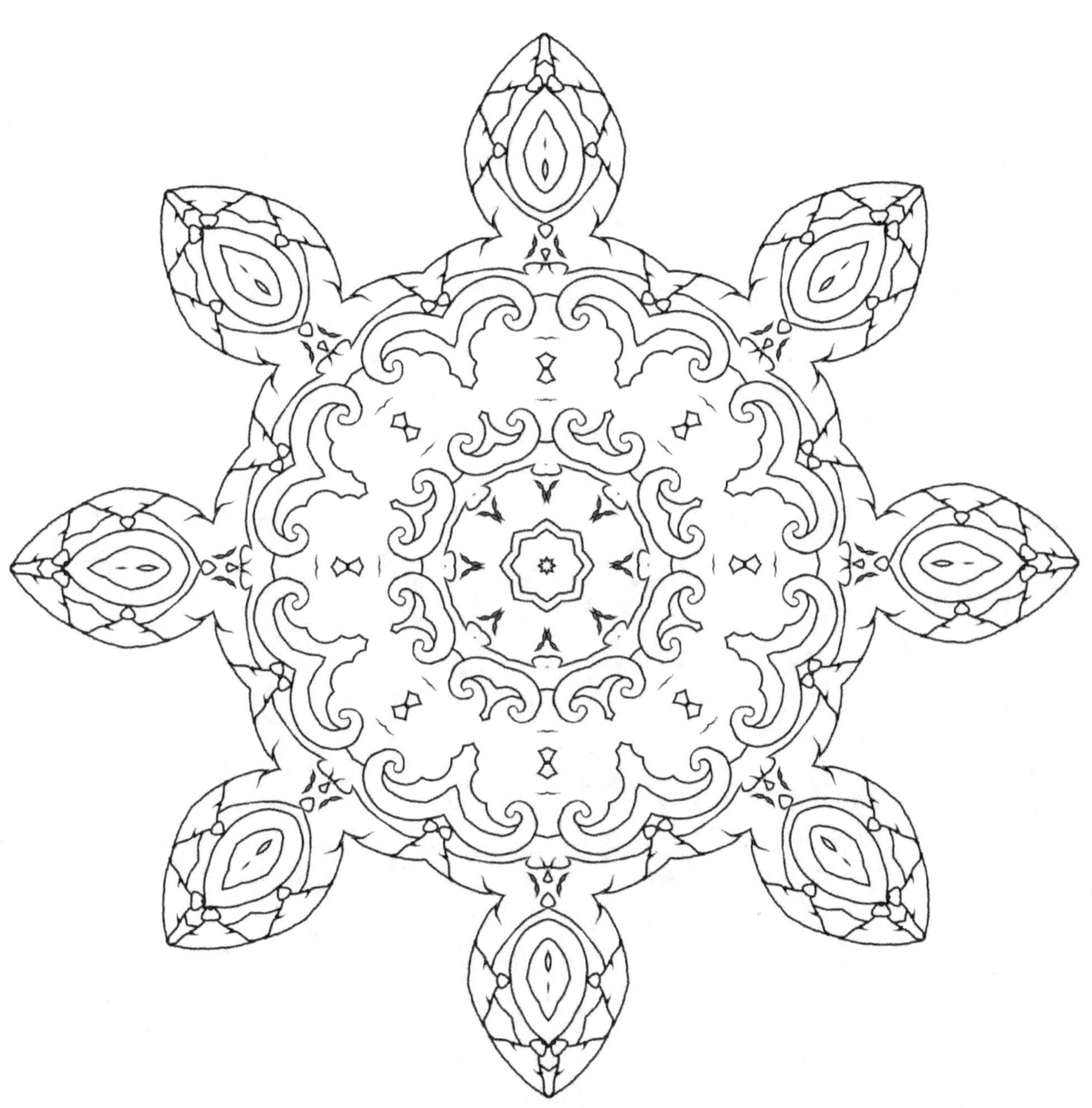

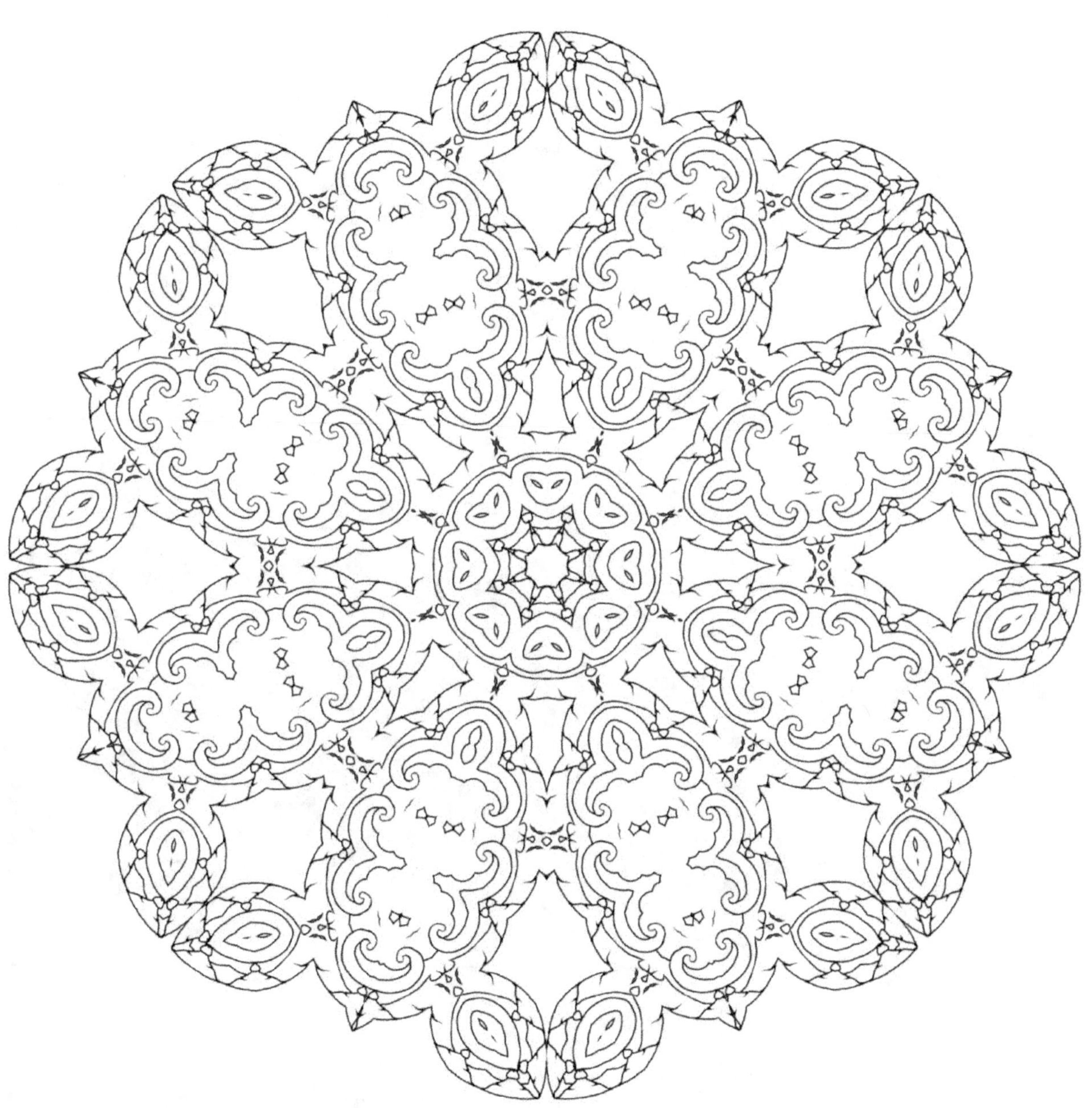

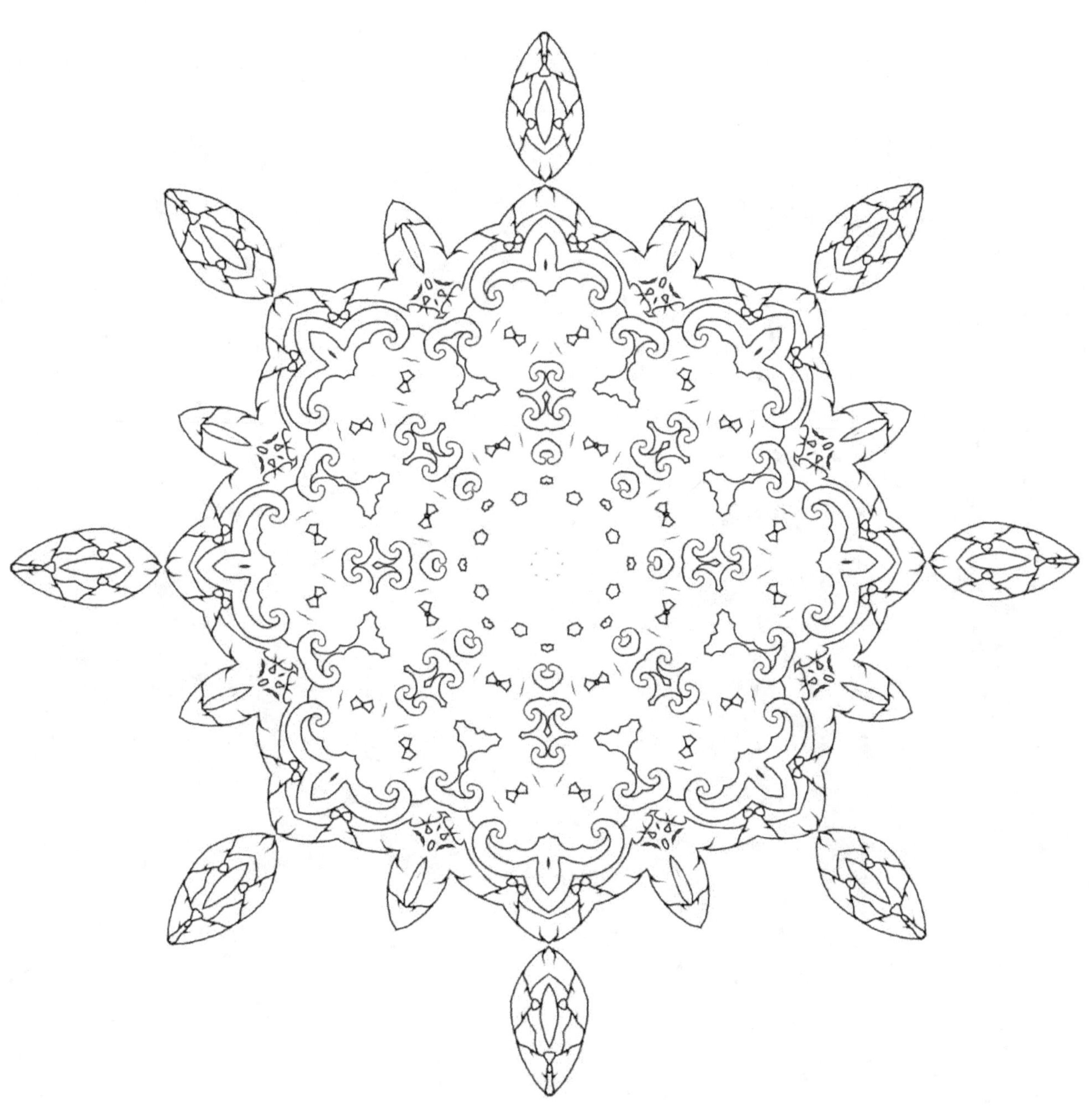

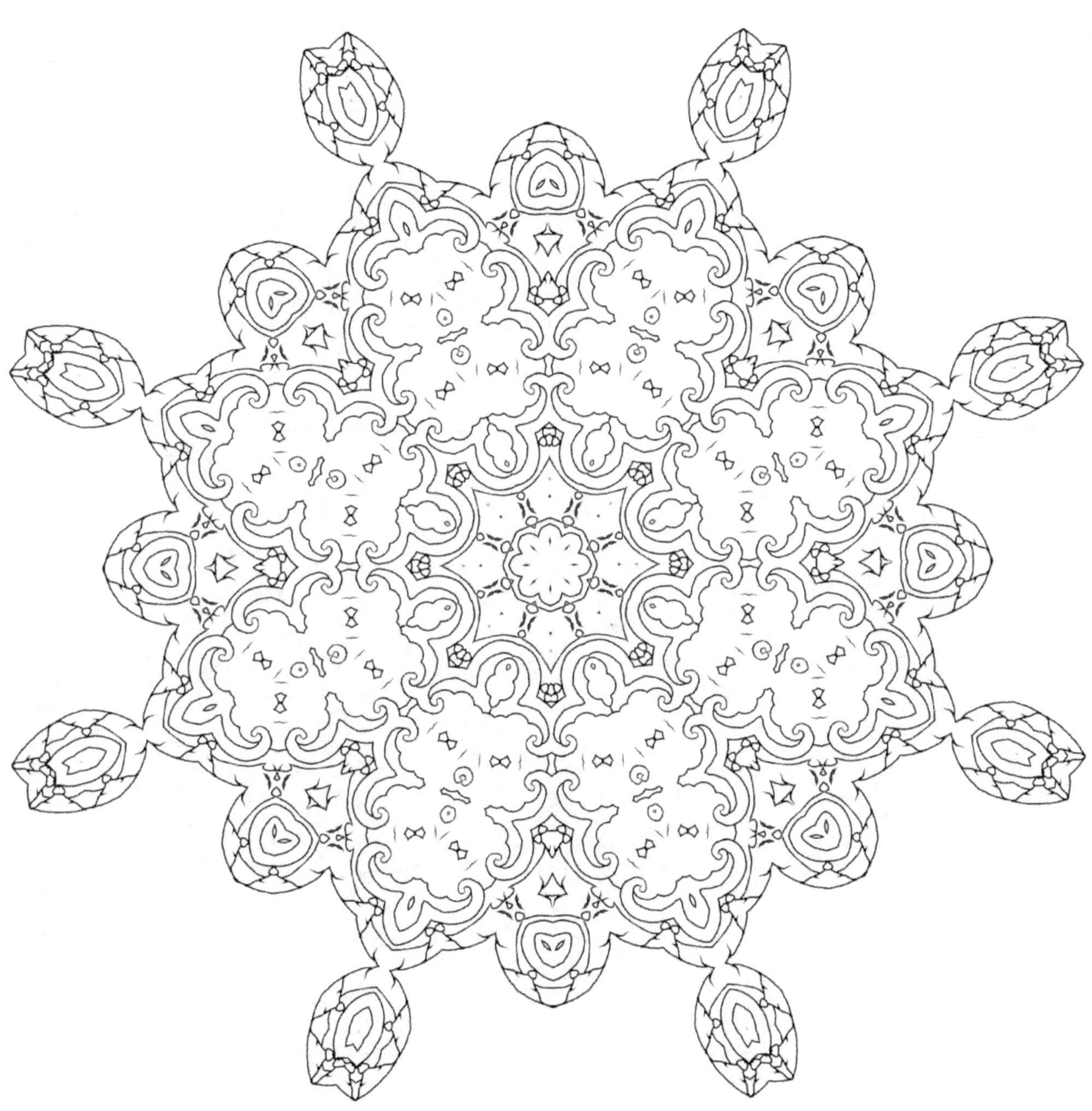

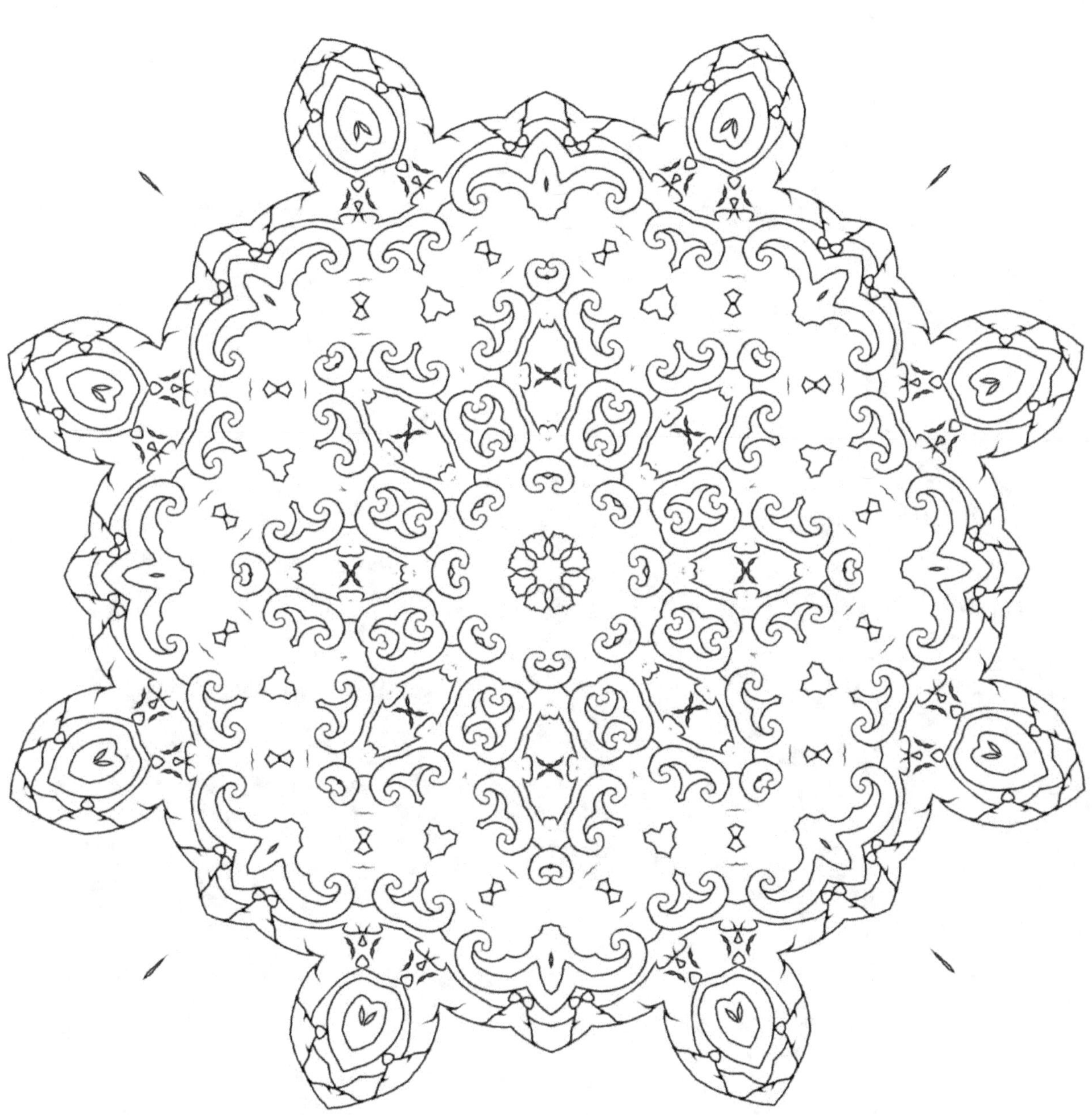

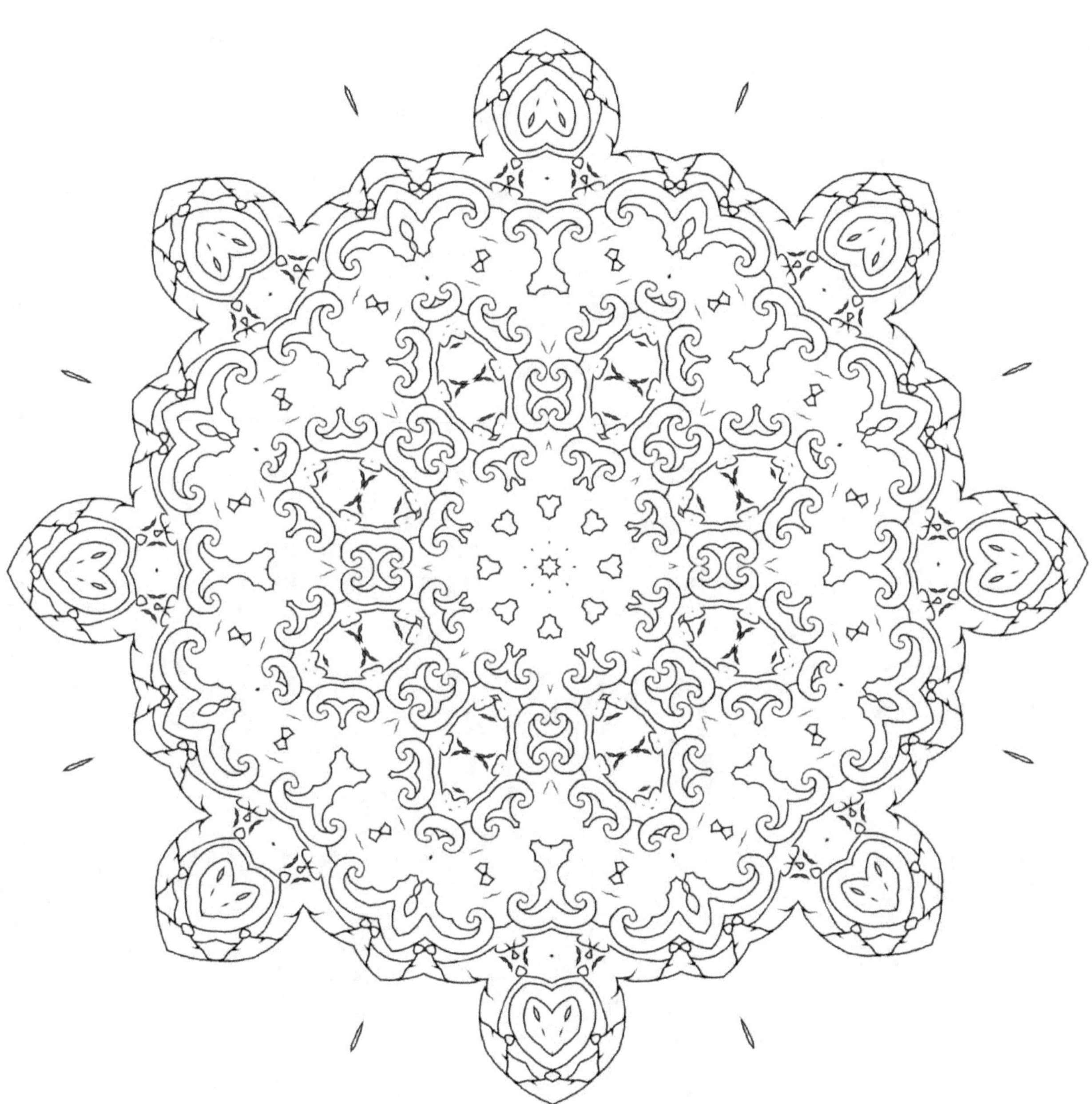

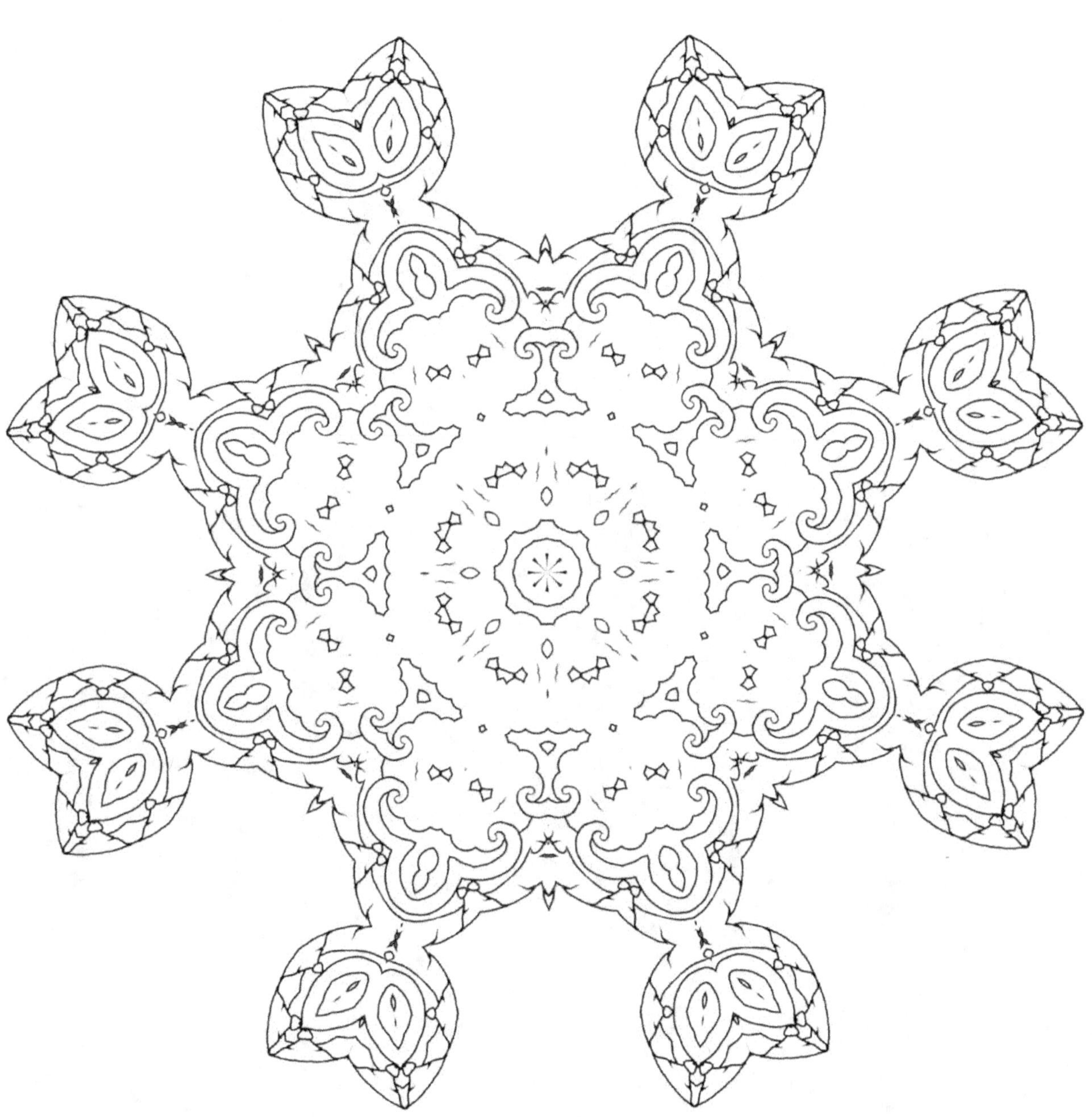

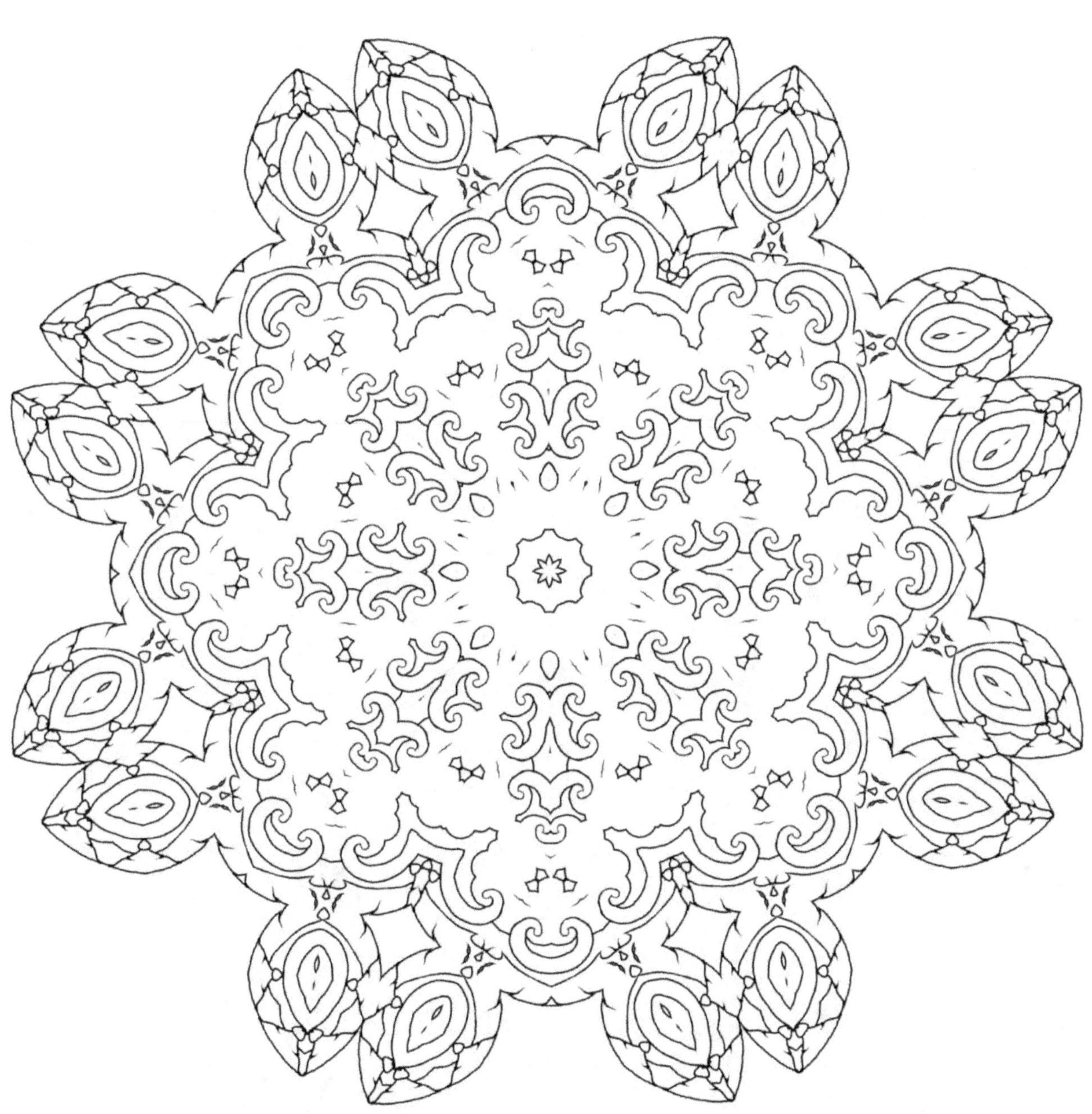

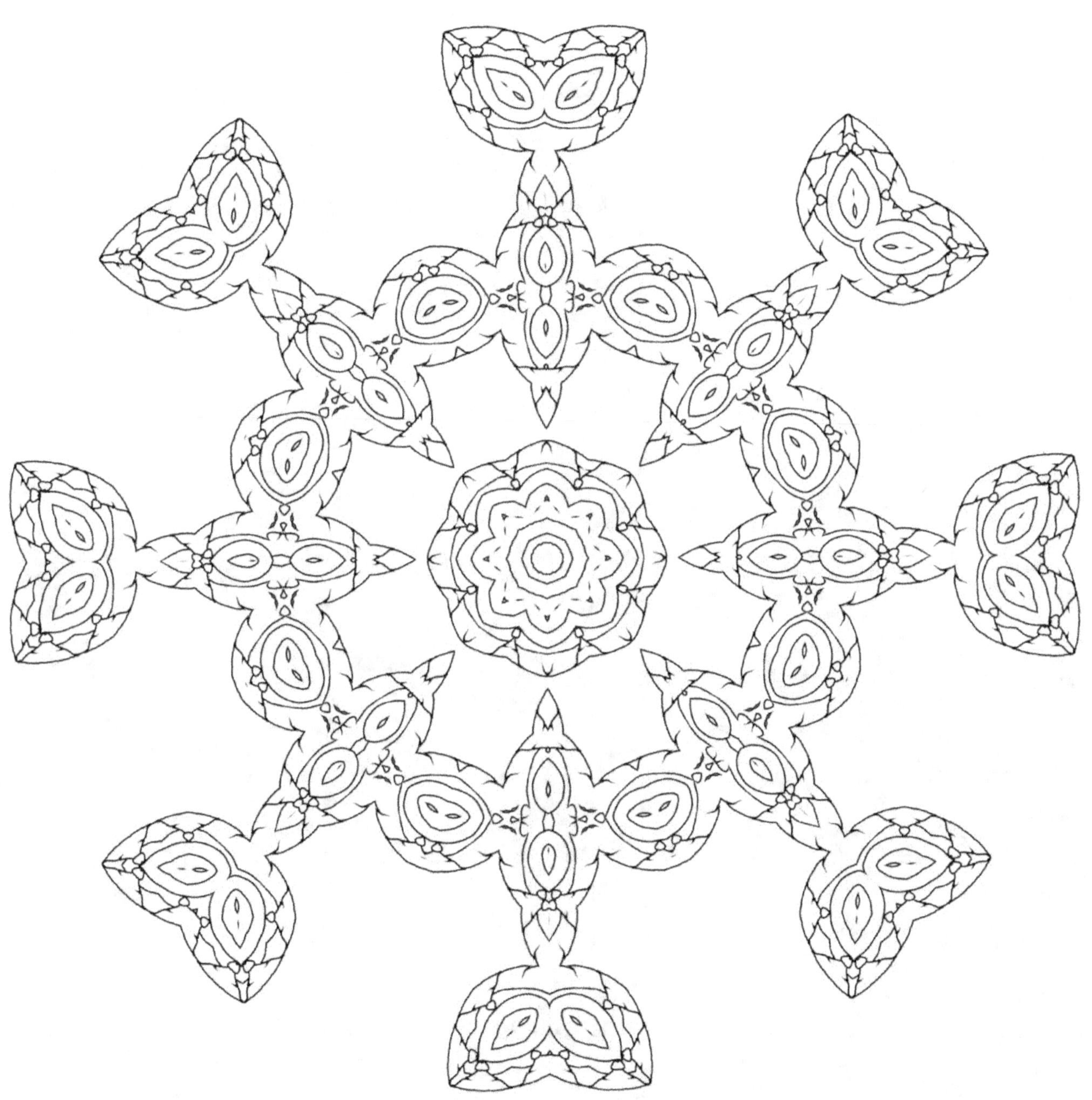

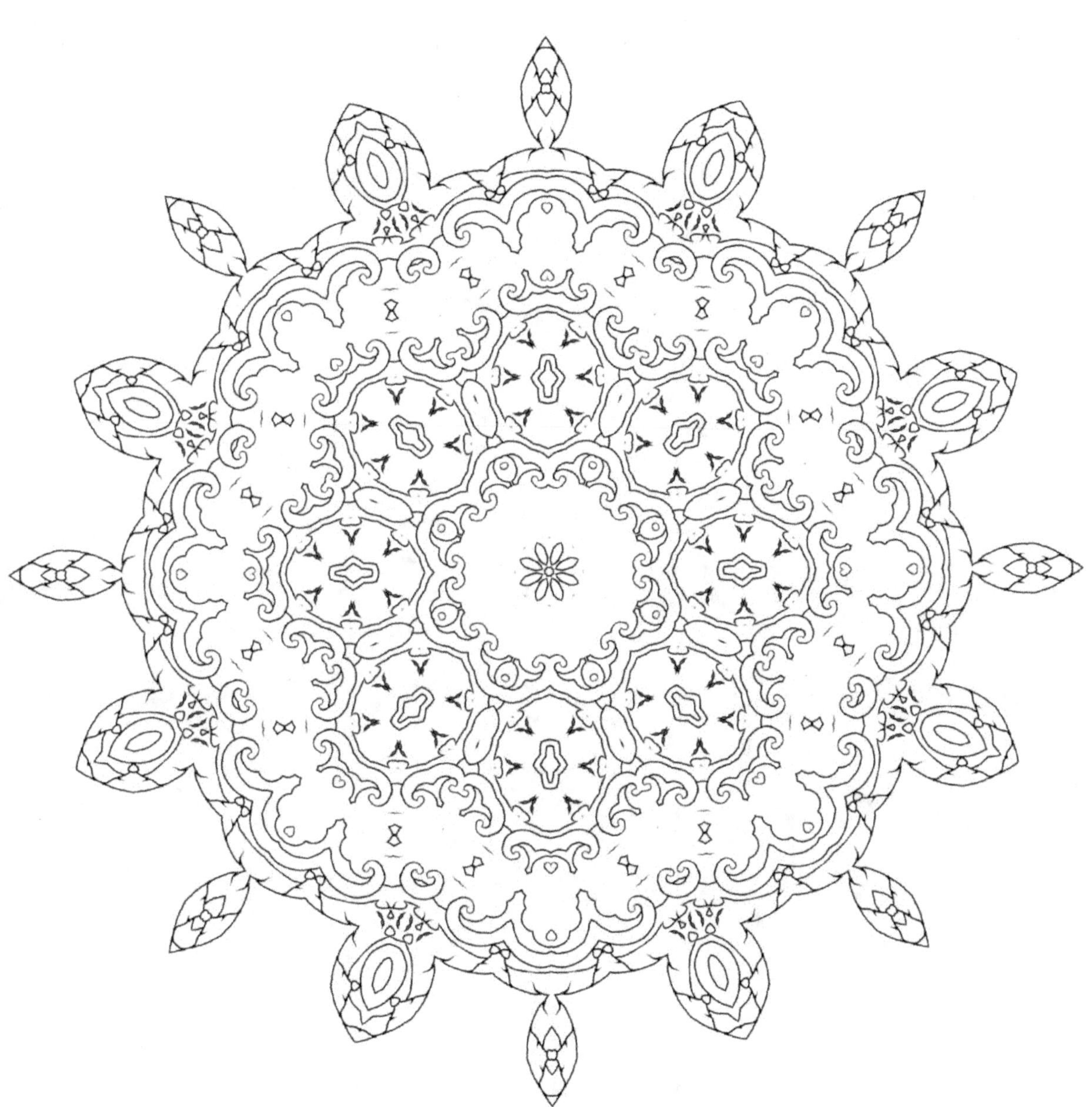

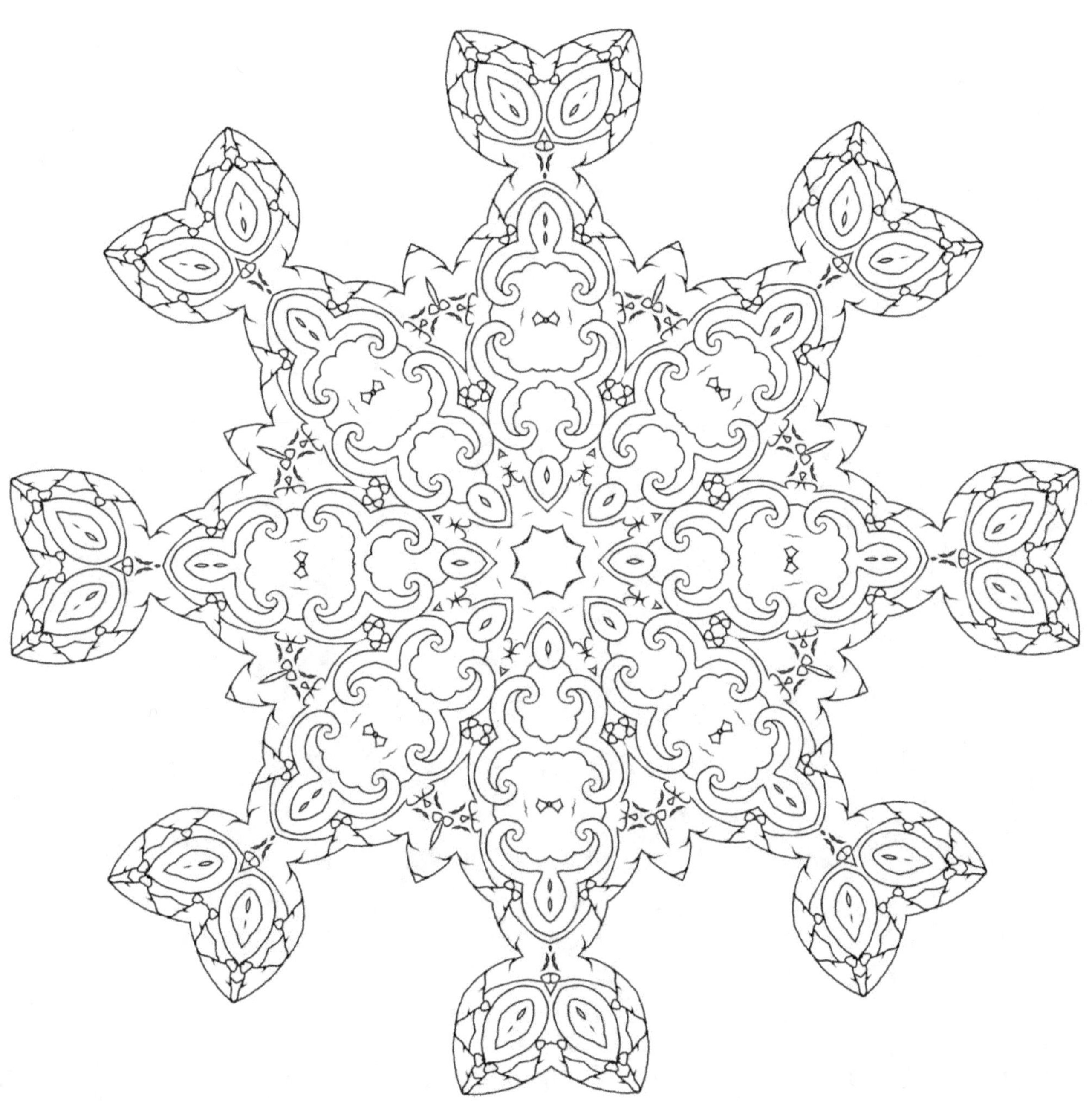

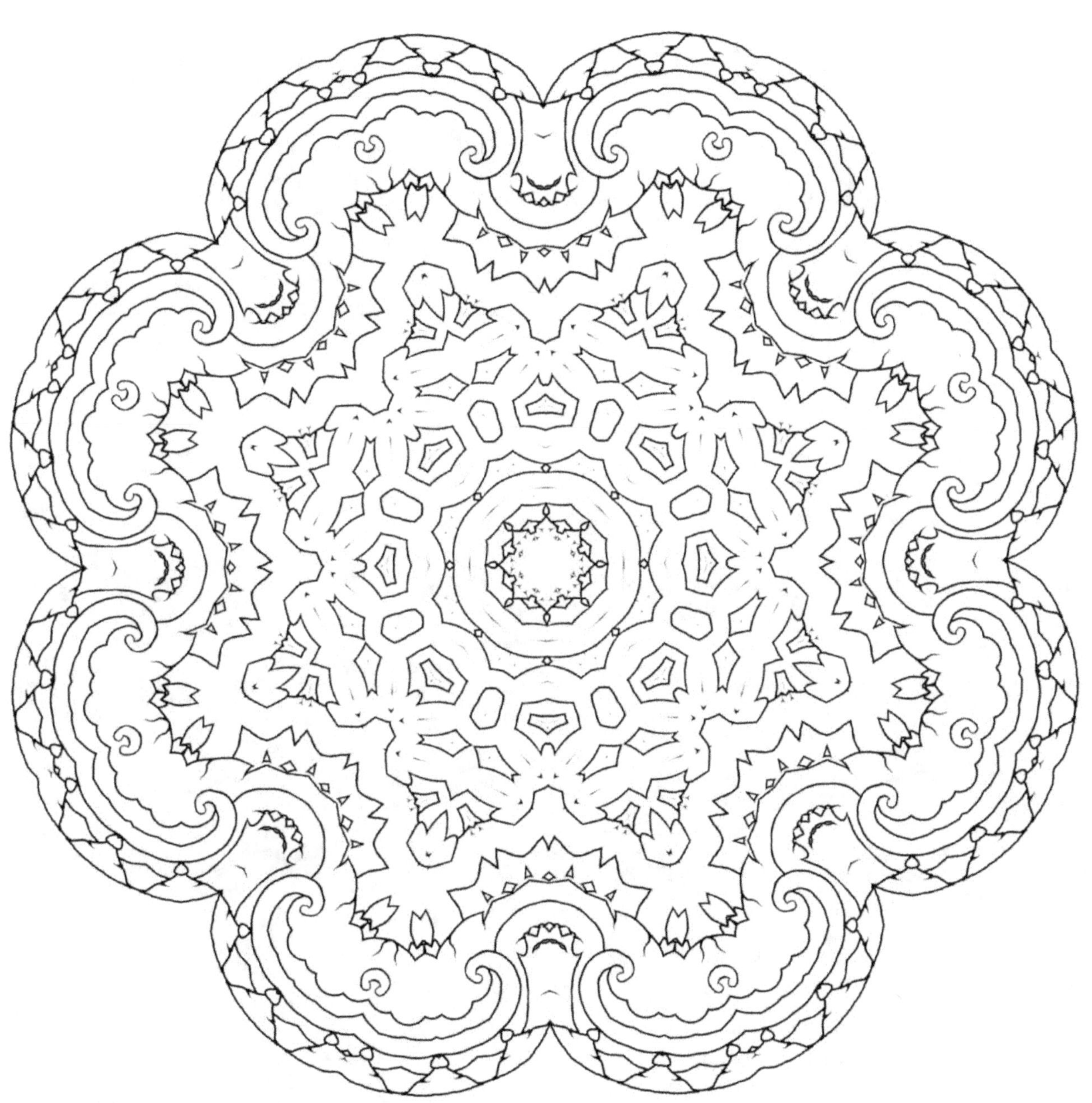

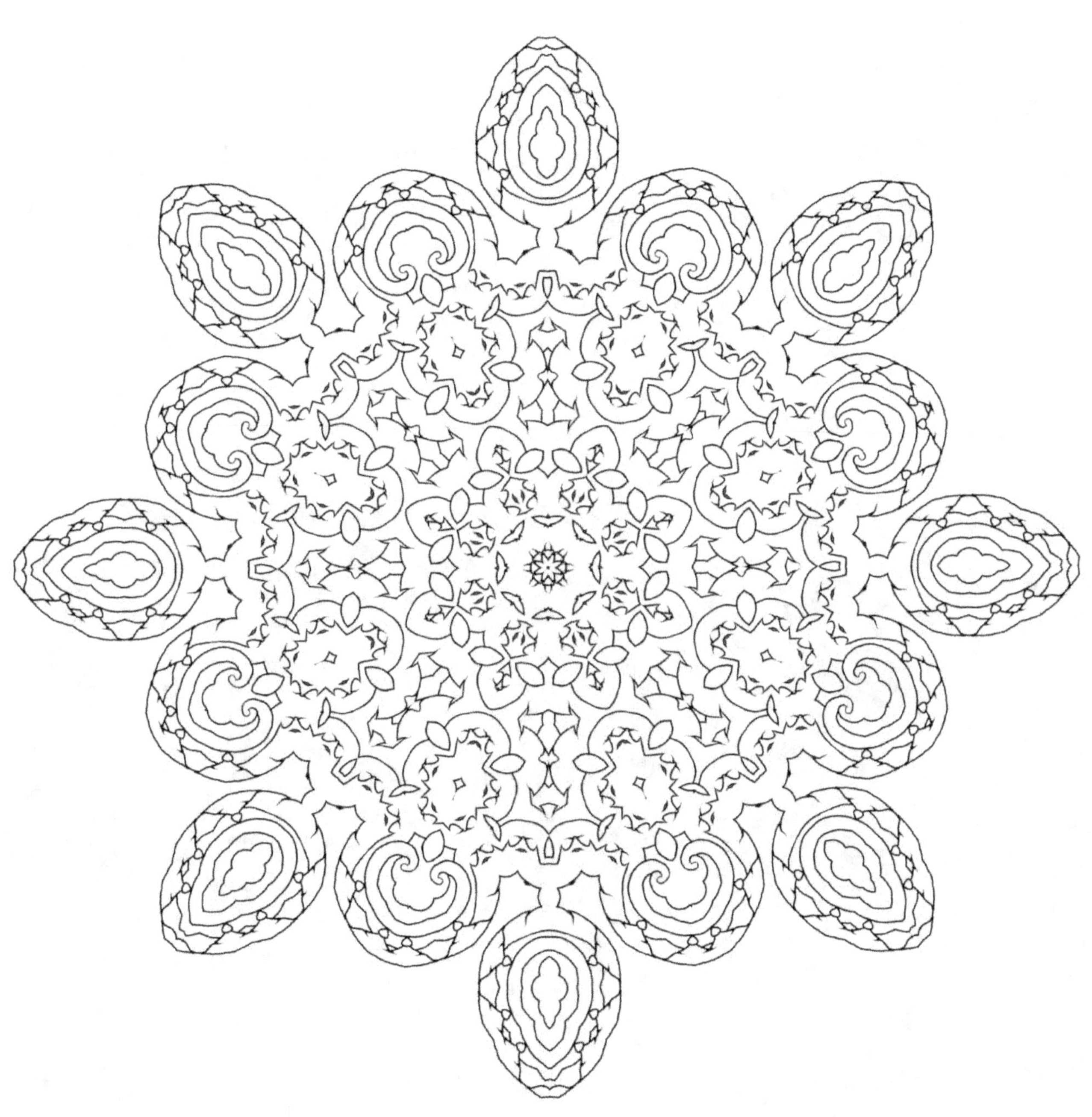

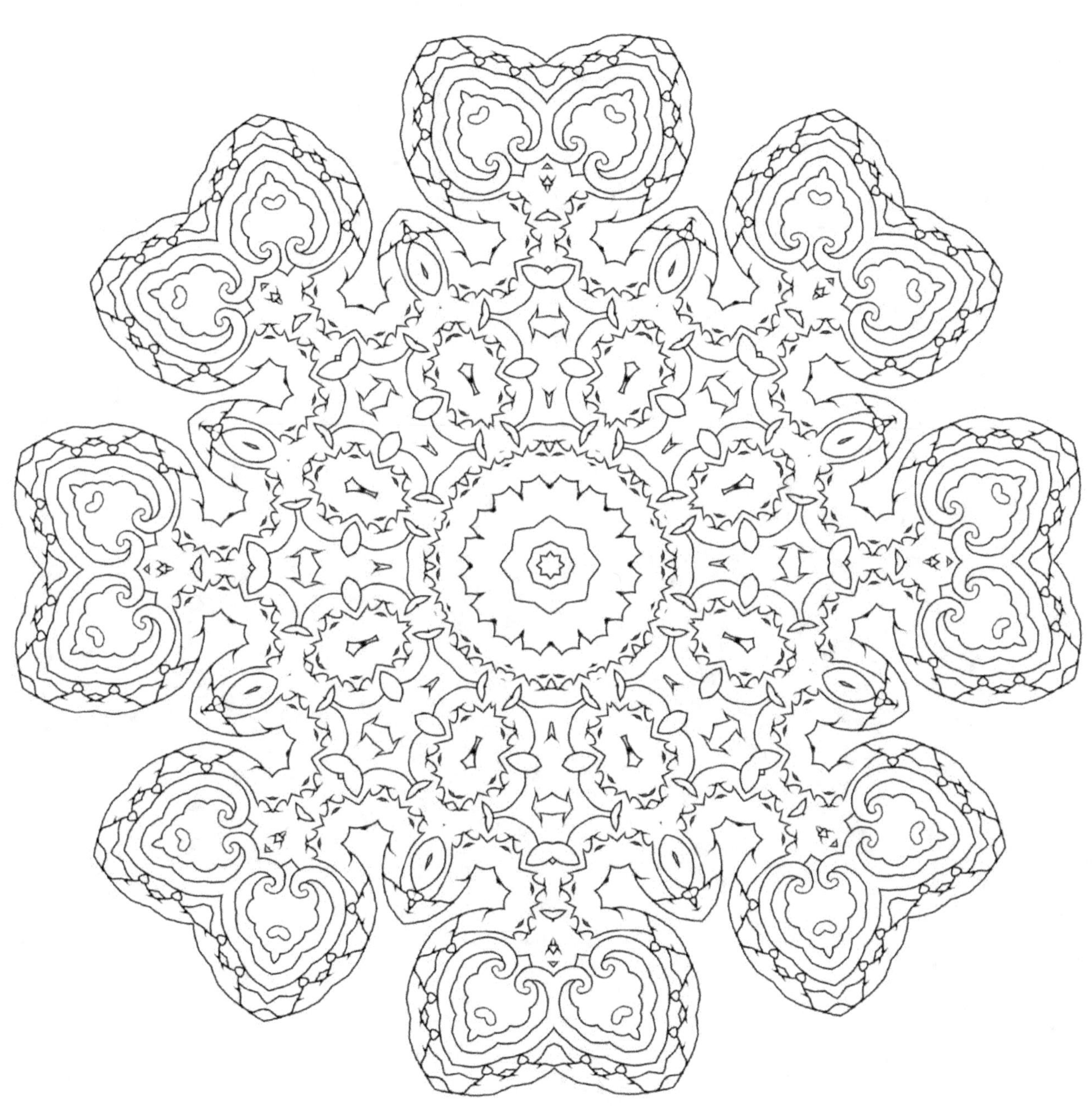

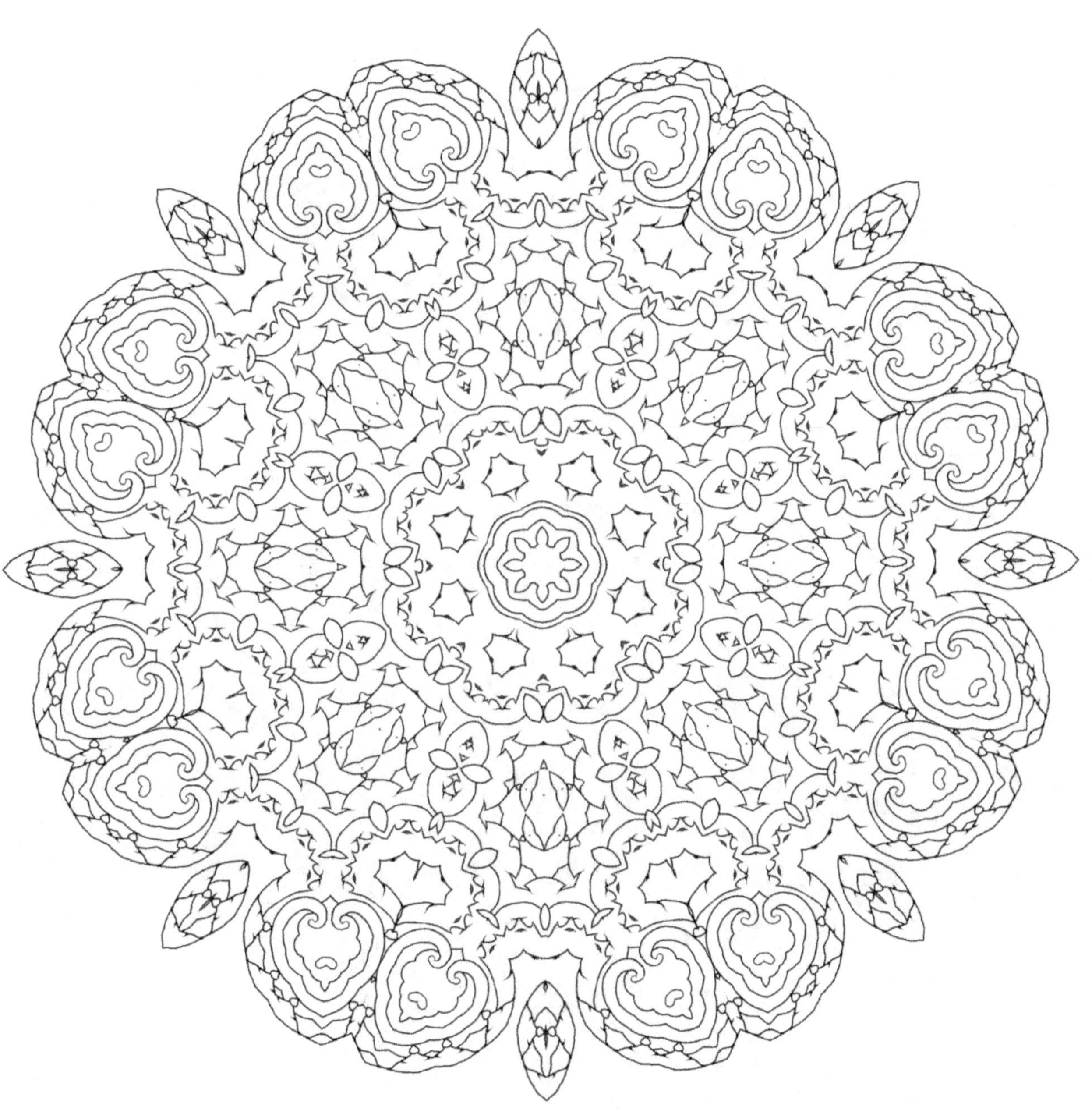

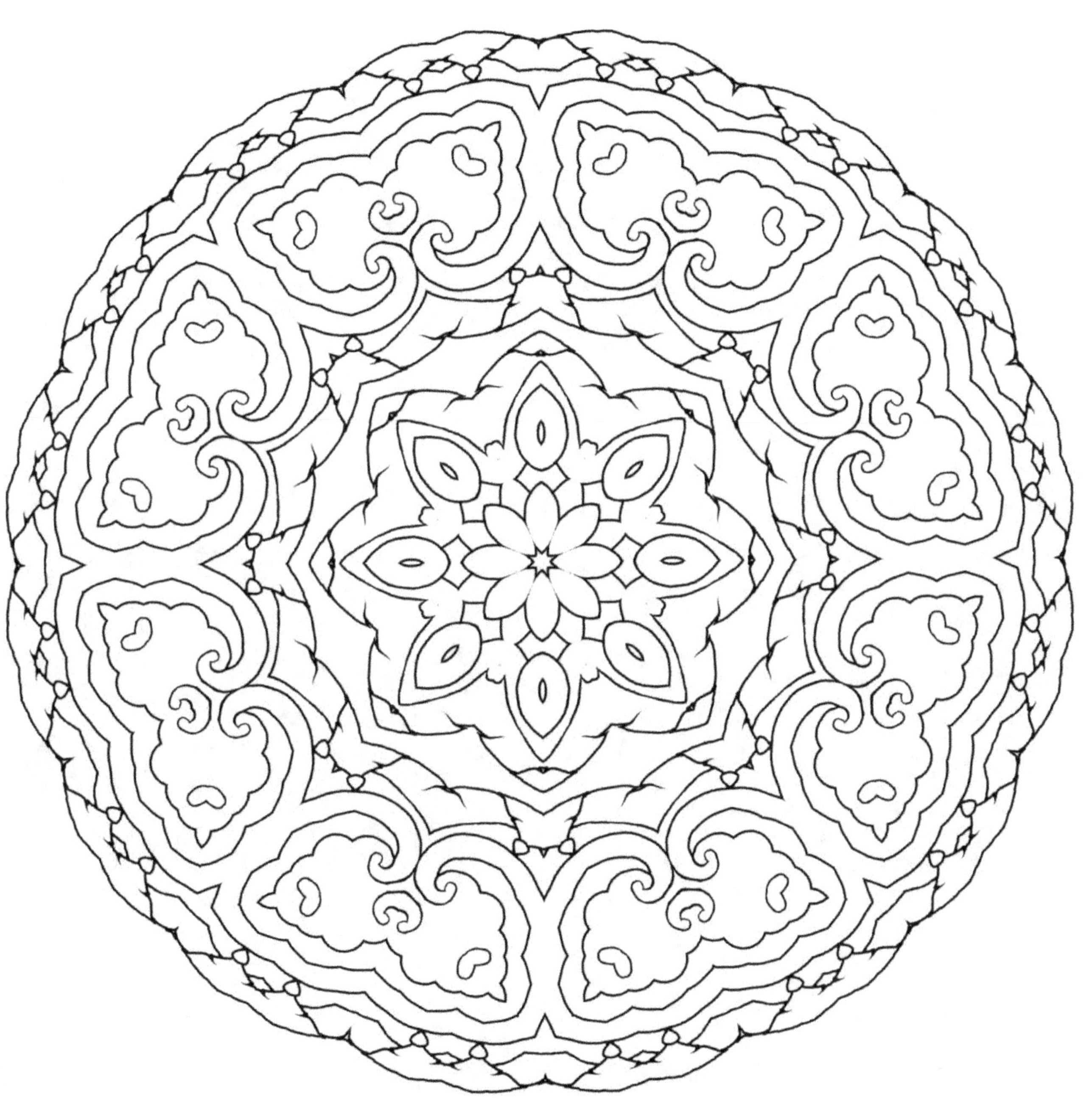

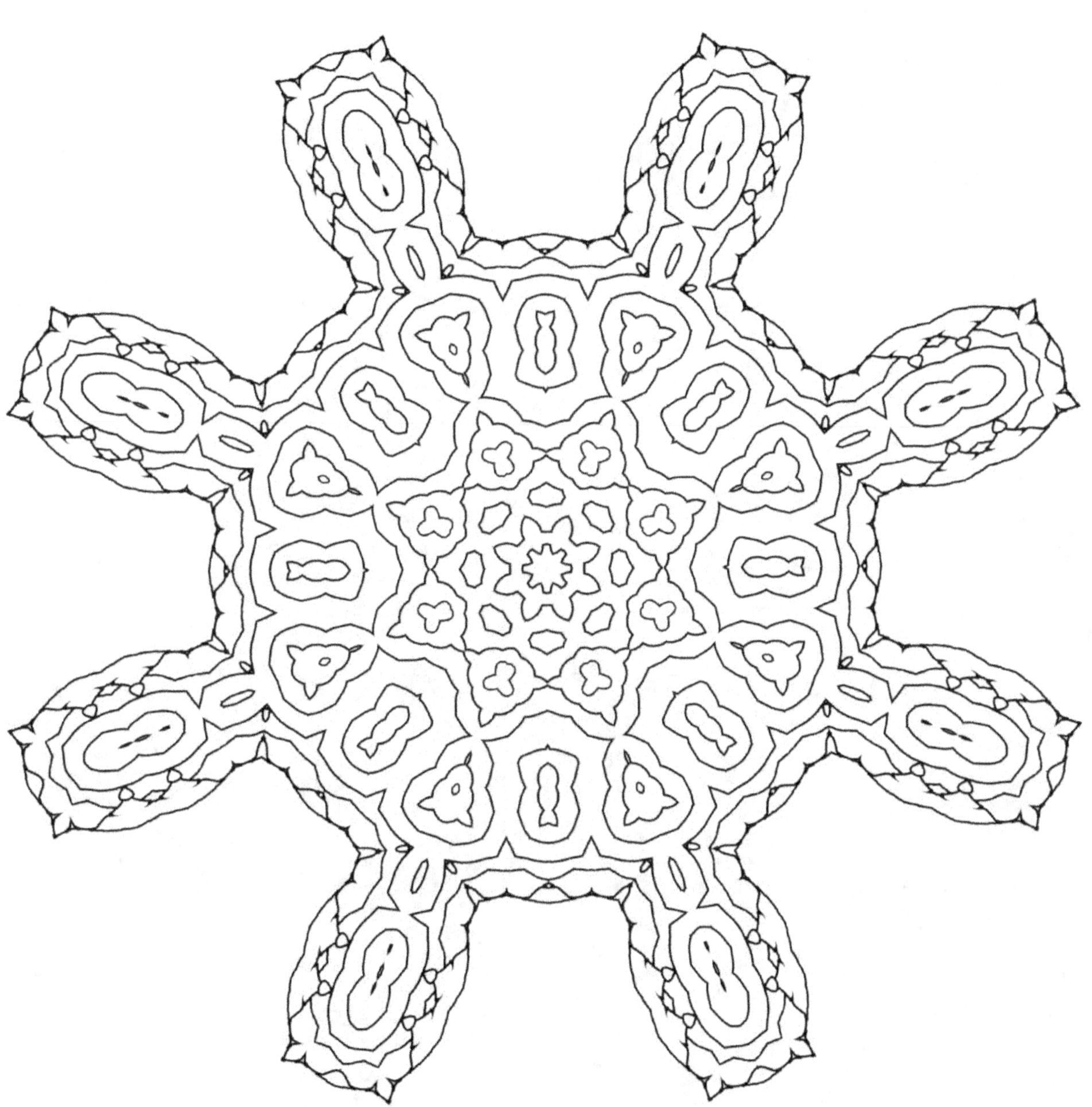

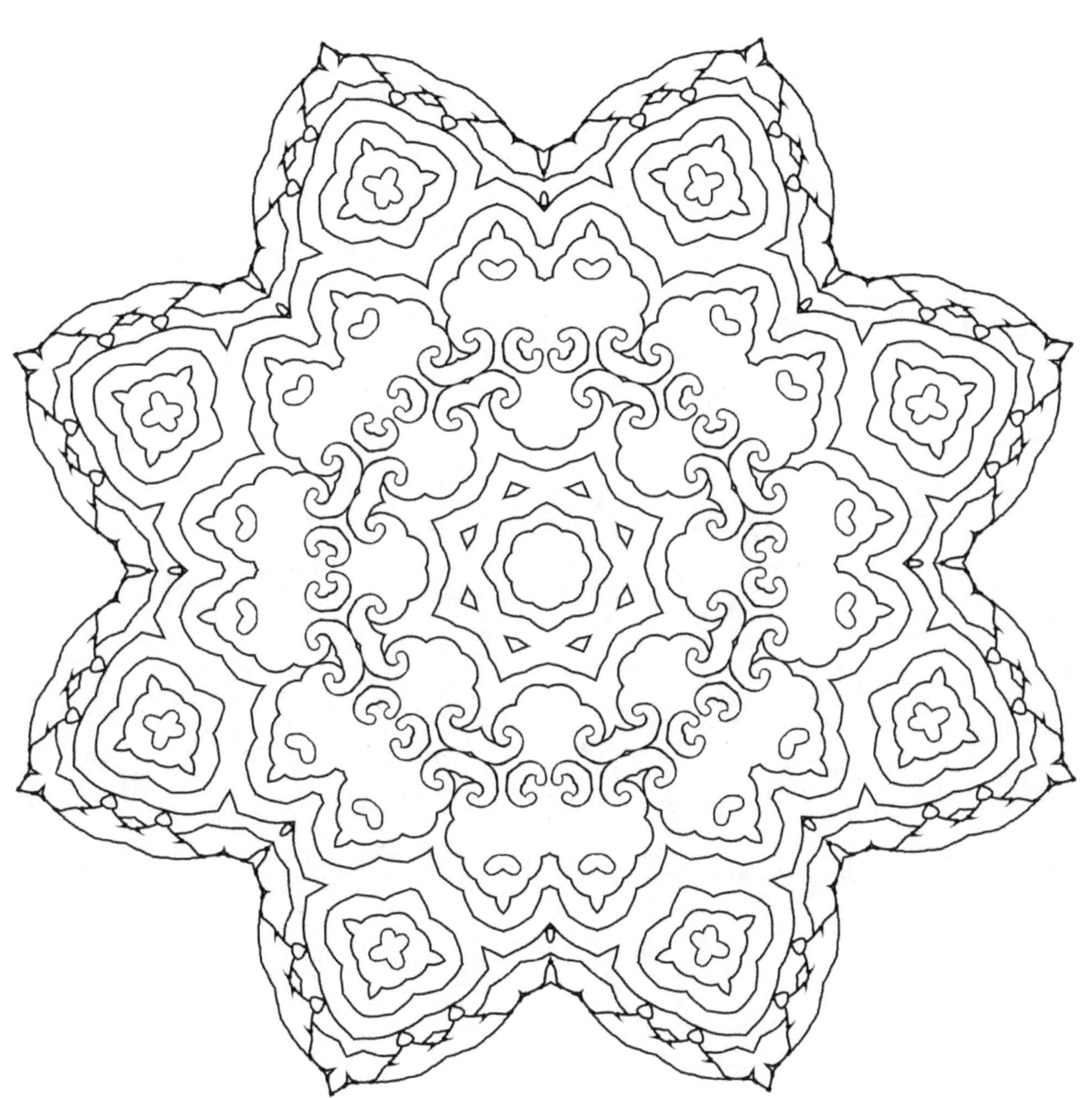

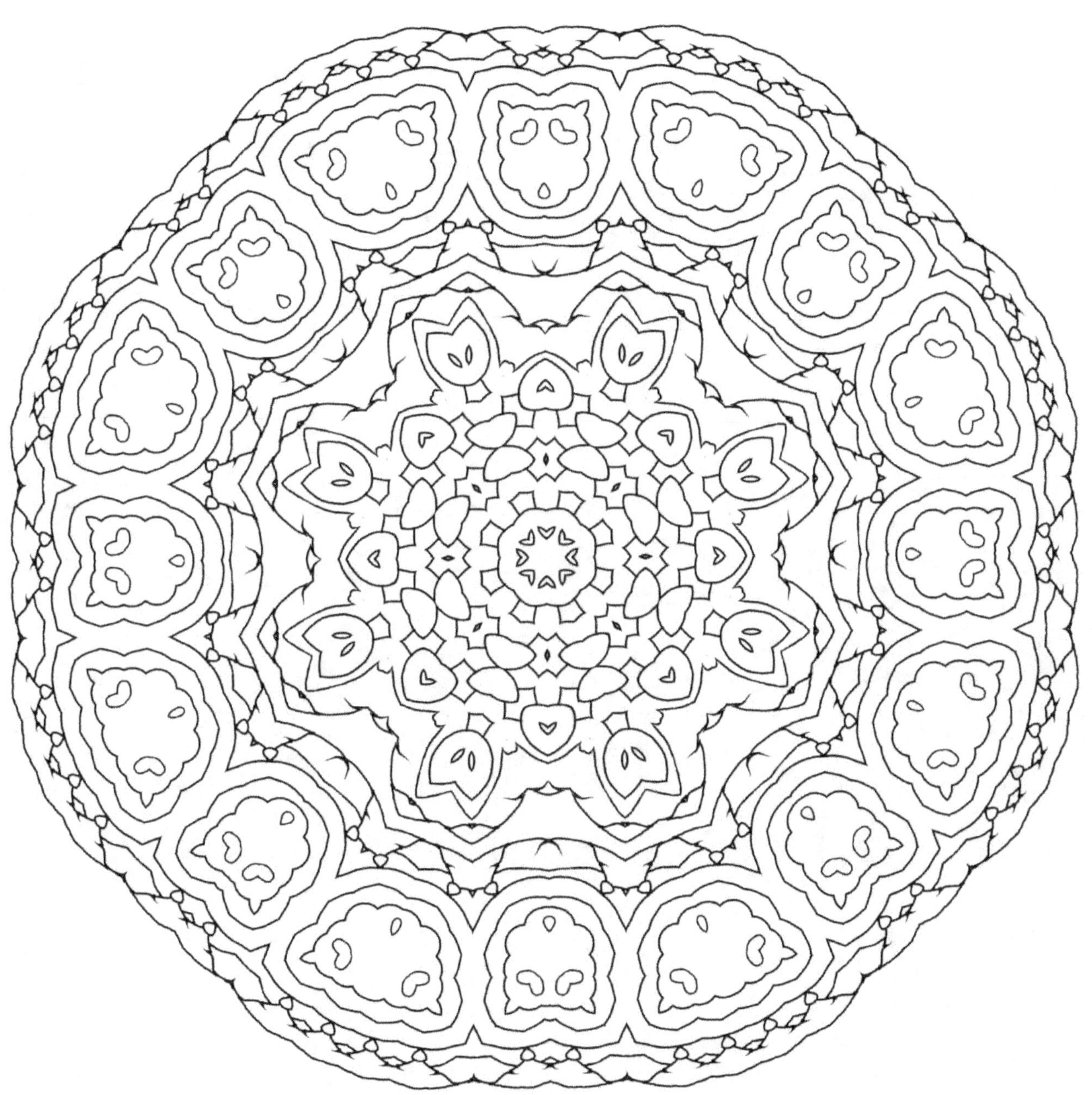

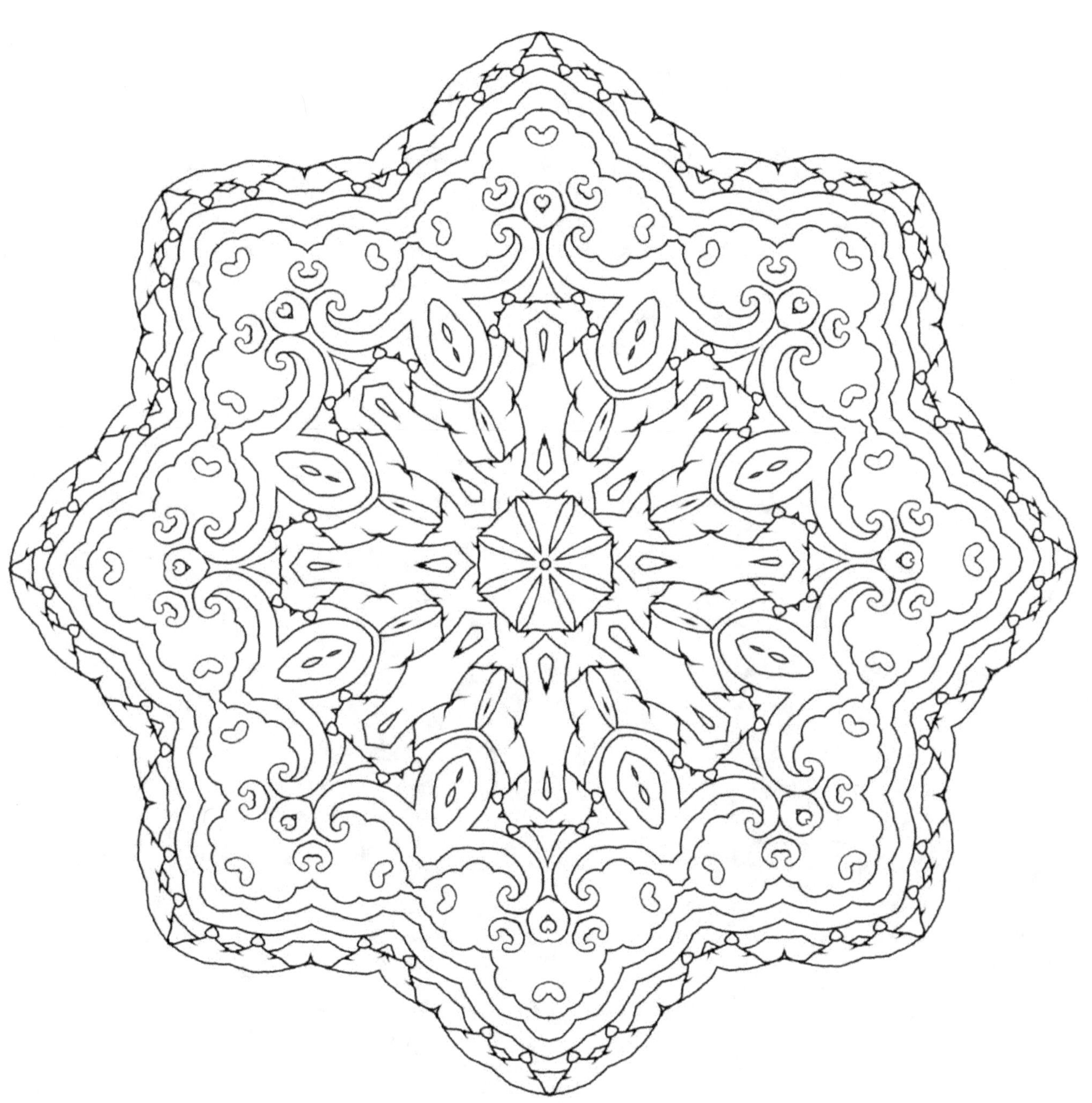

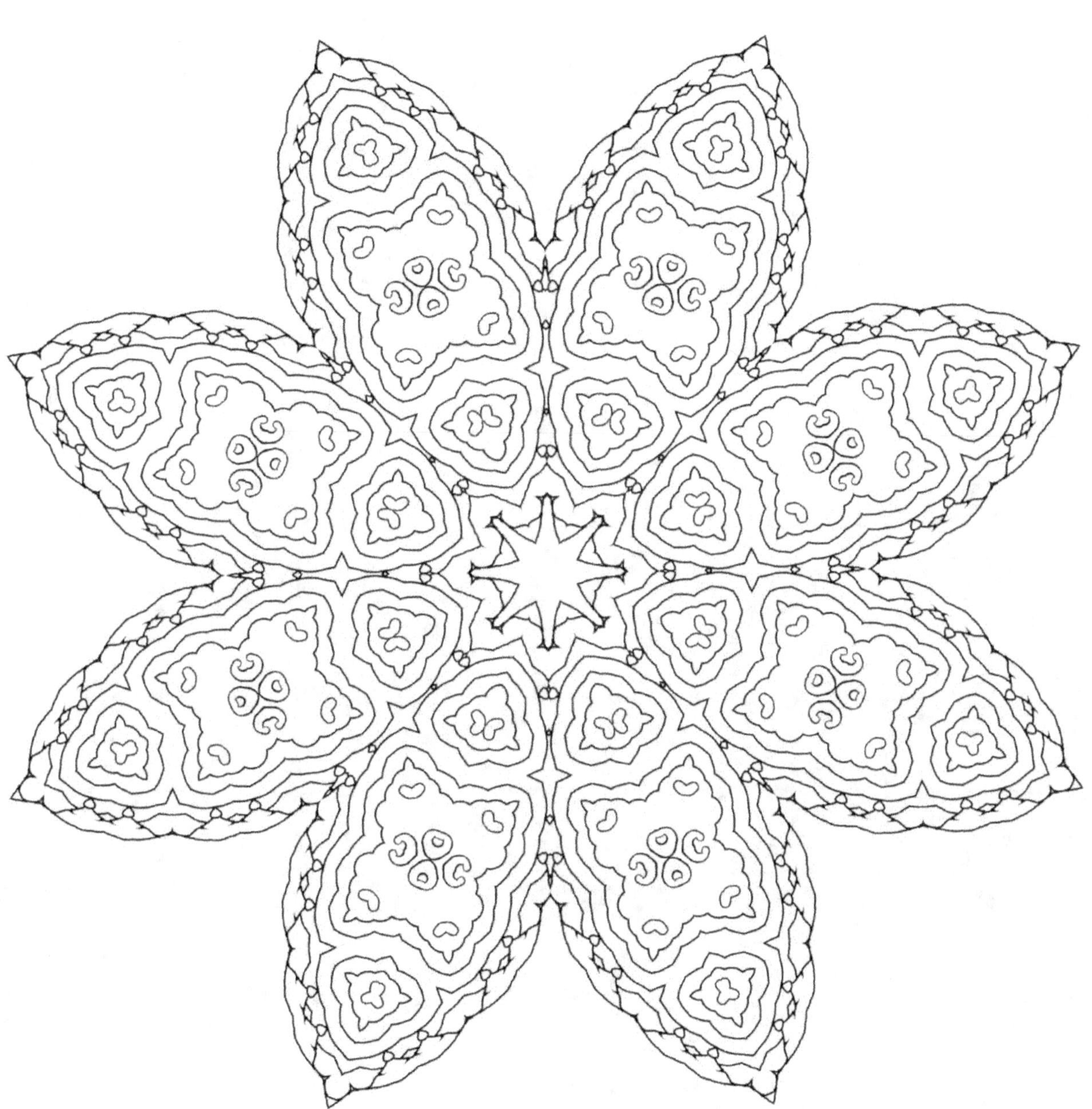

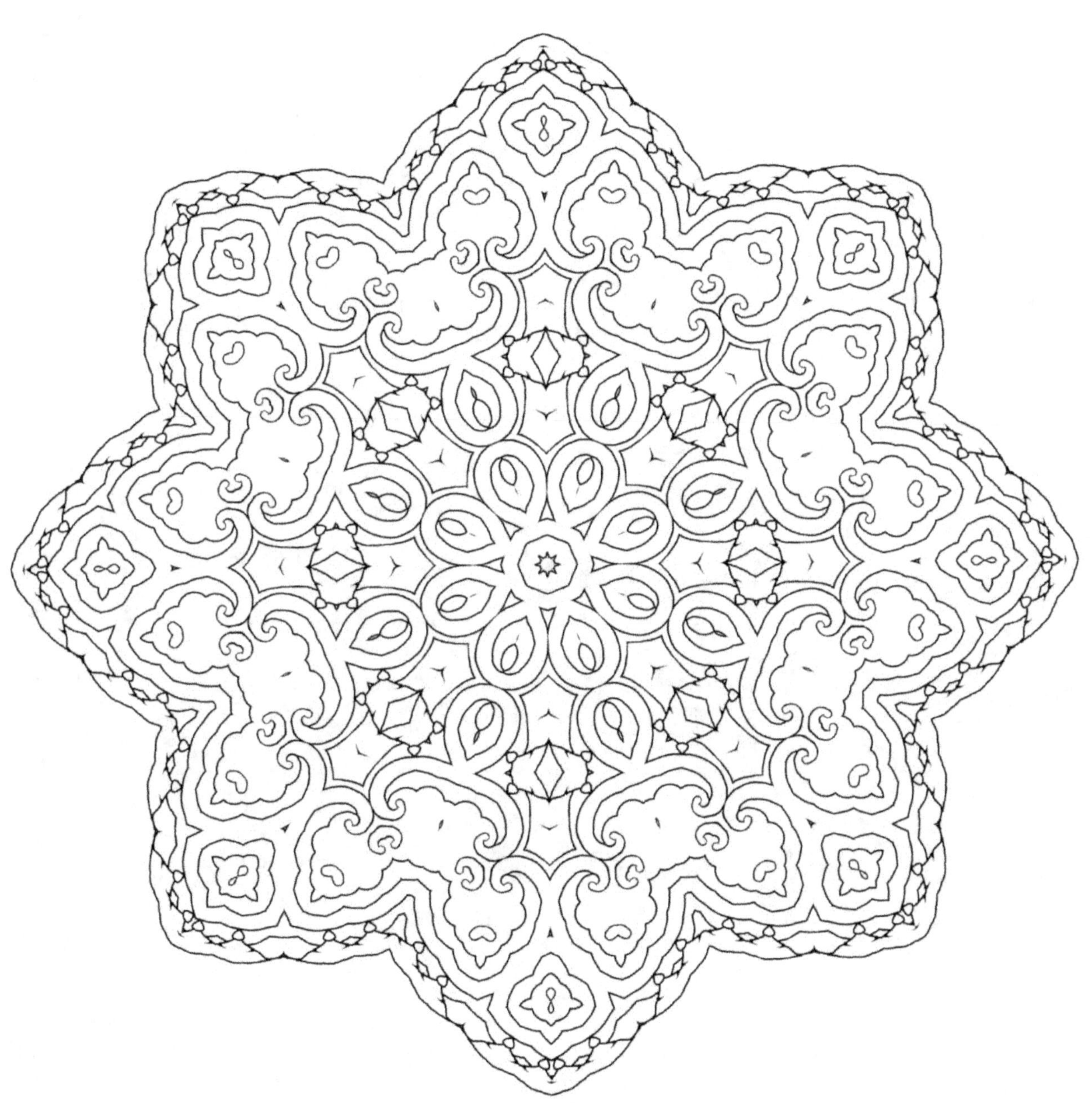

Thank you

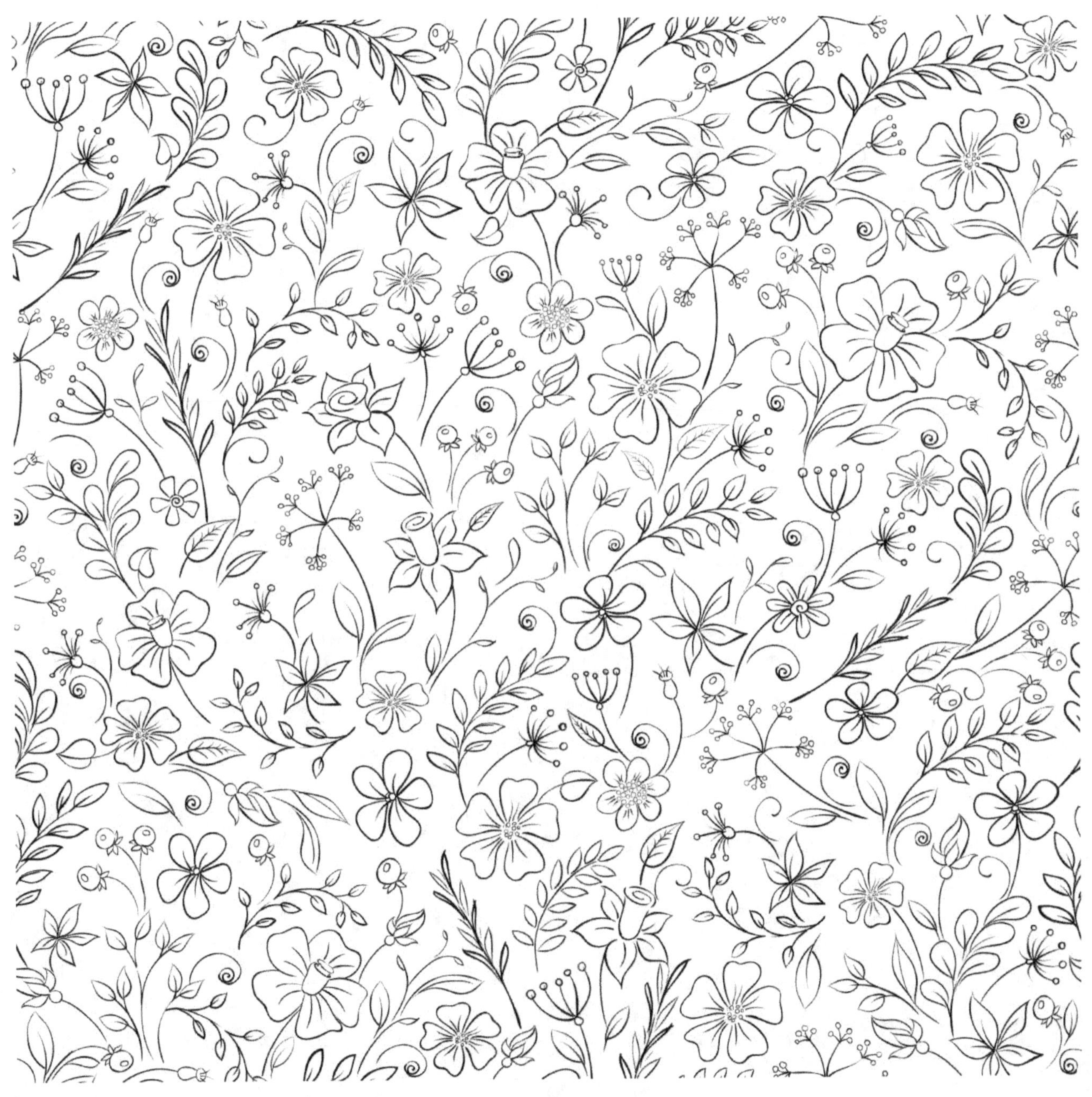

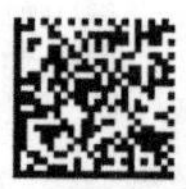

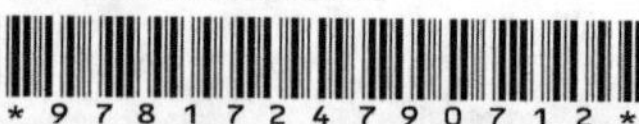
9 781724 790712